FamilyCircle

Dinner Parties

The Family Circle Promise of Success

Welcome to the world of Confident Cooking, created for you in the **Family Circle Test Kitchen,** where recipes are double tested by our team of home economists to achieve a high standard of success – and delicious results every time.

M U R D O C H   B O O K S®

Sydney • London • Vancouver

CONTE

Traditional Favourites, page 58.

Quick and Easy, page 82.

Italian Fiesta, page 14.

Seafood Celebration, page 44.

The Publisher thanks the following for their assistance in the photography for this book: Barbara's Storehouse; Corso de' Fiori; Cosmopolitan Stone; Home & Garden On The Mall; Les Olivades; Noritake; On Broadway Antiques; Paraphernalia; Waterford Wedgwood; Warwick Fabrics; Villeroy & Boch; Whitehill Silver. All suppliers in Sydney.

Brasserie-style, page 52.

Autumn Bounty, page 32.

The test kitchen where our recipes are double-tested by our team of home economists to achieve a high standard of success and delicious results every time.

When we test our recipes, we rate them for ease of preparation. You will find the following cookery ratings on the recipes in this book, making them easy to use and understand.

A single Cooking with Confidence symbol indicates a recipe that is simple and generally quick to make – perfect for beginners.

Two symbols indicate the need for just a little more care and a little more time.

Three symbols indicate these are special dishes that need more investment in time, care and patience – but the results will be well worth it.

Dinner Party Basics

A dinner party should be an occasion of enjoyment for guest and host alike. Here is how careful planning, fabulous food and wine and an eye to presentation will make your party a feast for all the senses.

Planning a Dinner Party

A well-planned party means that you and your guests can relax and enjoy yourselves. Gone are the days when rigid etiquette demanded a certain behaviour; modern dinner parties can be held on the terrace, by the pool, in the formal dining room or even in the kitchen, country-style.

Firstly, choose your guests, keeping in mind the number of people you, your dining table and your kitchen equipment can comfortably accommodate. Issue invitations, by phone or by letter for a formal occasion, at least two weeks ahead. Plan the menu and accompanying drinks and think about the table setting; make lists of tasks to be done ahead and on the day – this way you won't forget anything vital. Tick off tasks as you complete them. Shop well ahead, if possible, making good use of your freezer. Many liquor suppliers will deliver bottles and ice, even glassware.

On the day of your dinner party, lay the table, arrange flowers, chill wine; do everything possible so that last-minute tasks are keep to a minimum and when guests arrive you can greet them with a smile and without constantly disappearing into the kitchen. Your guests should feel comfortable, and if the host is relaxed the guests will be too. Keep that in mind and you can hardly go wrong.

Table setting for a three-course meal, with wine glasses to accompany each course. Cutlery is ranged to the sides of the plates; use outermost cutlery first.

Table settings

The table arrangements for your dinner party depend on the occasion you are celebrating. At a casual event a simple setting will suffice, and anything more elaborate would not be appropriate. However, for a formal gathering or celebration dinner, bringing out the silverware, the elegant china and the best crystal adds to the sense of occasion.

Laying the table: There are simple rules to follow. Firstly, place a generous-size cloth over the table. For a traditional, dressed-up dinner with the entrée or soup plate on top; side plate to the left. Close in to the dinner plate, place cutlery for the dessert course; working outwards, place main course cutlery, then cutlery for entrée or soup. Forks are to the left of the dinner plates; spoons and knives to the right, with the sharp edge pointing to the left. The butter knife is placed on the side plate, with the sharp edge also pointing to the left.

Some people put the dessert spoon and fork horizontally above the dinner plate. This can be convenient if your table is small. If you prefer (and if you

Table setting for soup and main courses. Place soup plate on dinner plate.

Alternative table setting for entreé, main course and dessert.

Table setting for dessert course. Clear plates and lay dessert plate and cutlery.

FEASTING THE EYES

Small personal touches can elevate your dinner table into a work of art. Co-ordinate the colours of flowers, cloth and napkins; a white and gold table scheme is classically elegant, while vibrant colours add sparkle. Take advantage of the seasons – pile the prettiest fruits onto a glass or silver cake stand; spray-paint vine or ivy leaves gold and drape them over the table; cut branches of spring blossoms, autumn leaves or dry summer grasses to arrange as centrepieces, keeping them well below eyeline. Take up and enlarge the theme of the occasion, e.g. decorations for a seafood dinner could include shells, starfish and driftwood as well as flowers.

Lighting sets the mood; candles are attractive and give a flattering, warm glow. Light should be soft but not dim, so that the colour and texture of the food can be appreciated and guests can see each other clearly.

To make butter shapes: Have the butter very cold. Slice and cut into shapes with biscuit cutters.

To make butter curls: Roll butter curler across a pat of very cold butter. Dip curler into hot water occasionally to make it slide easily and to prevent clogging.

1. To open a wine bottle: cut the top from foil cover and remove.

2. Insert the corkscrew straight down into the cork.

3. Twist the corkscrew down into the cork, using firm pressure.

4. Hook lever over the edge of bottle and lever cork out with the handle.

are serving the main course on warmed plates) lay the table with cutlery for the first two courses, and only the soup or entrée plate.

Wine glasses are placed just above the knives, and in order of use; the outermost glass is drunk from first. If you have three wines, place glasses in a triangle above the knives; the top glass is used last.

The Menu

The menus in this book are planned for you. They have been prepared according to several themes: following the seasons (taking advantage of fresh produce); the type of dinner party (casual, formal); a specific type of food (seafood, vegetarian); and regional cuisine (French, Italian). You can follow the menus as they are or mix and match recipes to suit your personal preferences. Aim for a good balance of flavour, texture and colour.

Offer your guests three or more courses – an appetiser, soup or entrée, the main course, a dessert and perhaps a sweet treat with coffee and liqueur.

When planning your menu, be aware of your skills as a cook. For beginners, a simple meal that you can easily prepare is the best option, but if you want to attempt a difficult dish, try one that can be made a day or two ahead. If disaster should strike, you'll have time to prepare another dish.

Decide what to serve with dinner. Bread comes in many shapes and sizes and in more colours than white or brown; try multi-coloured vegetable loaves, chunky cottage loaves, pretty knotted rolls or whatever seems appropriate to the meal. Serve rolls warm in a napkin-lined basket; place loaves on a breadboard with a knife to cut at the table, or slice it beforehand. Coffee can be served with or after dessert. Plunger or brewed coffee is best.

Liquid Refreshments

There are many intimidating rules about presenting and drinking wine, but the serving of wine at your dinner party should not cause a problem. Rules are made to be broken; let your personal preferences and taste be your guide. Wine bottles can be placed directly on the table, kept cool in an ice-bucket or wine cooler or decanted into a carafe or other pretty container.

1. To open champagne: remove foil cover from around the cork top.

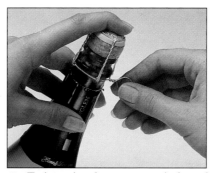

2. Twist wire loop to unwind and remove the wire cage completely.

3. Gently loosen the cork by pushing with your thumbs.

4. Cover the top of bottle with a napkin and remove cork.

Your guests may also appreciate the offer of cold mineral or soda' water. Serve water in a wine goblet.

Wineglasses: Wine experts agree that the shape of the glass effects the taste of wine; that's why they come in varying shapes and sizes. Good wines should be served in fine crystal glasses. Champagne and other sparkling wines are served in a tall flute glass to preserve the bubbles. Serve white wine in a long-stemmed wine glass and red in a shorter, bigger-bowled version, to let the wine 'breathe'. Potent liqueurs and other fortified wines can be served in tiny glasses and are meant to be sipped, because of their high alcohol content. Finally, whatever the shape of the glass, don't overfill it. Half to two-thirds full is plenty.

Opening the wine bottle: The most important thing to know about opening a bottle of wine or champagne is that it should be done smoothly, and without fuss. Never pull a wine cork out with force There are many corkscrews and wine openers on the market. The corkscrew in the step-by-step photographs, (see previous page) known as a 'waiter's friend', has a blade for cutting the foil over the cork and a lever to help pull out the cork. Other types of corkscrew are just as effective. The only ones you should avoid are those that remove the cork through brute strength.

To use the waiter's friend, cut the top from the foil cover on the neck of the wine bottle with the blade. If your corkscrew doesn't have a blade, use a sharp knife. You need only remove the top of the foil, not the whole cover. Insert corkscrew into the cork. Ensure that the corkscrew goes directly down the centre of the cork, otherwise the cork may break when you pull it out. Twist the corkscrew into the cork, hook lever over the edge of the bottle and lever the cork up to remove.

Cloths and napkins

A simple damask or linen cloth and matching cloth napkins, lightly starched, pressed and prettily folded, are a beautiful foundation for your table. Lace cloths give an old-fashioned air; white is classic; plain colours and prints can be contemporary, rustic or romantic. If your table is likely to be marked, place a blanket or felt cloth under the tablecloth.

Decorative napkins: Folding napkins into attractive shapes is not difficult. For best results begin folding with the napkin placed in front of you with the hemmed edges of the napkin

To make Formal Dress: roll the first layer down from the top.

Champagne

Champagne and sparkling wines are fun to open because there's such a feeling of celebration about it. Open bottles gently and quietly, producing a subtle pop. Never push the cork so that it explodes out and hits the ceiling, or a guest, and liquid spurts over the cloth.

To open champagne: Remove foil wrapping from around the top of the cork. Twist the loop of wire to unwind and lift off the wire cage. Gently loosen the cork by pushing with your thumbs or with your hand, using a screwing motion as if unscrewing a jar. Partially remove the cork, cover the top of the bottle with a napkin; smoothly and firmly twist cork out.

To pour champagne: Pour in two motions. Tilt glass, then pour in champagne until glass is half full. Wait a few seconds until the foam subsides, then pour again until the glass is two-thirds full.

1. To make Elegant Ruffles: turn the first layer down from the top corner.

2. Pleat this folded layer accordian-fashion. Finish with point downwards.

3. Place a heavy glass to hold pleats and pleat the second layer.

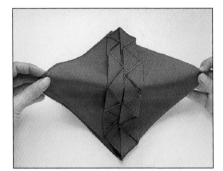

4. Turn the napkin so pleats are vertical and fold napkin in half.

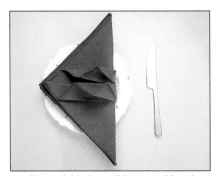

5. Place folded napkin on side plate; place butter knife beside plate.

(if any) running horzontally at top and bottom and selvedges vertical.

A basic napkin ring fold: Fold the napkin into quarters and place it in a diamond shape in front of you, with the folded corner at the bottom. Fold the right point towards the centre and overlap with the left side, until a sharp point is formed at the bottom of the napkin. Turn the napkin over, squeeze the long part together and slip a napkin ring almost up to the centre.

Simple Bow Tie: Fold the napkin into quarters and place in a diamond shape in front of you, with the open point at the left. Beginning at the bottom, pleat napkin, accordian-style, to the top. Hold folds in place, insert into a napkin ring. With ring at the center, fan out folds at either end. Place across plate to resemble a bow tie.

Simple Lacy Points: (This style is good for lace-edged napkins.) Fold the napkin into quarters and place it in a diamond shape in front of you, with the closed corner at the top. Starting at the bottom point, take the first layer of napkin and bring it up to meet the top point. Bring the second layer of the bottom point to within 2 cm of the top point. Repeat with remaining layers, folding each layer a little further down

so that each edge shows and all are spaced evenly apart. Press with your hand to hold folds, if necessary. Place the napkin flat on the dinner plate.

Elegant Ruffles: (see step-by-step photographs above). Fold the napkin into quarters and place in a diamond shape in front of you, with the open corner at the top. Turn the first layer down from the top corner to make a fold in the middle. Pleat the folded layer accordian-fashion, with the point finishing downwards. Sit a heavy object on the fold to keep it in place. Pick up the second layer from the top and pleat it exactly as the first row of pleats. Lightly iron or press folds firmly with hands to keep their shape

without making them flat. Turn the napkin so the pleats run vertically. Hold outside corners and fold napkin in half. Place napkin on side plate.

Formal Dress: (see step-by-step photographs below). Fold napkin into quarters and place in a diamond shape in front of you, with the open corner at the top. Roll the first layer from the top corner down, so the top of the roll is at the centre. Fold down next two layers, tucking each a little under previous rolls to hold. Smooth rolls with your hand. Turn the napkin around to a square, and fold the top and bottom edges under to make a rectangle with the folds running diagonally. Place napkin on side plate.

2. Roll down the next two layers in the same manner.

3. Turn napkin and fold the top and bottom edges under.

4. Place the folded napkin vertically on the side plate.

FRENCH BISTRO

ENTRÉE: Tomato Garlic Mussels

MAIN: Veal with Wine and Mustard Sauce

ACCOMPANIMENT: Herbed Potatoes

DESSERT: Crème Brûlée with Plums in Lime

SWEET TREAT: White and Black Truffles

TOMATO GARLIC MUSSELS

Preparation time: 15 minutes
Cooking time: 10 minutes
Serves 6

18 large green-lip mussels
40 g butter
3 cloves garlic, crushed
3 large ripe tomatoes, chopped
1 tablespoon Worcestershire
  sauce
2 tablespoons tomato paste
¼ cup apple juice

➤ PICK OVER mussels and discard any with damaged shells.

1 Remove beards from mussels and wash away any grit. Discard one half of the mussel shell, leaving the meat attached to one side.

2 Melt butter in large heavy-based pan. Add garlic; cook 1 minute or until golden. Add tomatoes, Worcestershire sauce, tomato paste and apple juice and stir over medium heat 2 minutes. Bring mixture to boil, reduce heat. Simmer, uncovered, for 5 minutes.

3 Add mussels; cover and simmer a further 5 minutes or until mussels are tender. Serve with salad greens.

COOK'S FILE

Storage time: The sauce for this dish can be cooked ahead of time and stored, covered, in the refrigerator. Cook mussels just prior to serving.

Variation: This recipe can also be made with scallops or prawns.

Wine suggestions: Choose French wines for this menu: a light red is the perfect partner for mussels; with the veal, white burgundy (ideally serve the same wine as used in the recipe); and with the crème brûlée try a sweet dessert wine. Or, for a more casual event, serve a full-bodied chardonnay or white burgundy throughout the meal.

Crème Brûlée with Plums in Lime (top) and Tomato Garlic Mussels.

VEAL WITH WINE AND MUSTARD SAUCE

Preparation time: 10 minutes
Cooking time: 20 minutes
Serves 6

6 (about 140 g each) veal steaks
½ cup plain flour
1 teaspoon ground mustard
   seeds
50 g butter
2 teaspoons oil
1 cup white wine
⅔ cup chicken stock
3 teaspoons seed mustard

➤TRIM MEAT of fat and sinew.
1 Combine flour and ground mustard seeds on a sheet of greaseproof paper. Toss meat in seasoned flour; shake off excess. Reserve 3 teaspoons of seasoned flour.
2 Heat butter and oil in a large, heavy-based frying pan. Add steaks to pan. (Unless you have a very large pan you will have to cook them in batches.) Cook meat over medium-high heat 3 or 4 minutes each side. Remove from pan; drain on absorbent paper and keep warm. Repeat with remaining steaks.
3 Add combined wine, stock, mustard and the reserved seasoned flour to pan, stirring to incorporate any browned bits off the bottom of the pan. Stir until mixture boils and thickens. Place veal on serving plates, pour sauce over and serve with Herbed Potatoes.

COOK'S FILE

Storage time: Cook this dish just before serving.
Variation: Replace the seed mustard with any other style of mustard if desired. This recipe can also be made using six chicken breast fillets instead of veal steaks.

1

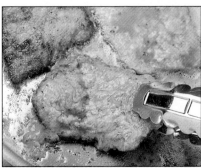

2

3

HERBED POTATOES

Preparation time: 20 minutes
Cooking time: 10 minutes
Serves 6

12 small new potatoes
80 g butter
2 teaspoons finely chopped
   fresh oregano

2 teaspoons finely chopped
   fresh thyme

➤WASH POTATOES thoroughly, removing any traces of dirt.

1 Cook potatoes in a medium pan of boiling water until just tender; drain. Transfer potatoes to medium mixing bowl. Keep warm.

2 Heat butter in a small, heavy-based pan on medium heat until it turns a nutty brown colour. Do not let butter burn. Remove from heat, stir in herbs.

3 Pour butter and herb mixture over potatoes, toss through gently and serve immediately.

COOK'S FILE

Storage time: Cook this dish just before serving.

Variation: Use any combination of fresh herbs from the garden.

1

2

3

CRÈME BRÛLÉE WITH PLUMS IN LIME

Preparation time: 1 hour
Cooking time: 1 hour + 10 minutes
Makes 6

3 cups cream
2 vanilla beans
8 egg yolks
½ cup caster sugar
1 teaspoon vanilla essence
3 teaspoons sugar

Plums in Lime
825 g can pitted plums
⅓ cup lime juice
⅓ cup sugar
zest of 2 limes, finely grated

➤ PLACE CREAM and vanilla beans in a large, heavy-based pan. Bring to boil; remove from heat. Set aside to infuse. Remove vanilla beans, rinse and retain for another use.

1 Beat or whisk egg yolks and sugar in large heatproof bowl until thick and pale. Place bowl over pan of simmering water; beat constantly until mixture is just warmed through. Add cream gradually to egg mixture, beating for about 10 minutes. Continue to stir until mixture thickens slightly and coats the back of a wooden spoon. Remove from heat, stir in essence. Spoon the mixture into six ⅔-cup capacity heatproof dishes. Refrigerate until set, about 2 hours.

2 To make Plums in Lime: Combine all ingredients in a medium,

heavy-based pan. Stir over low heat until sugar has completely dissolved. Bring to boil, reduce heat and simmer, stirring occasionally and keeping plums whole, for 40 minutes or until liquid has reduced and thickened. Remove from heat, set aside to cool.

3 Thirty minutes before serving, sprinkle ½ teaspoon sugar over each custard. Place custards into a large baking dish. Pack ice around the sides to prevent the custards being heated. Place under a pre-heated hot grill until sugar darkens and caramelises on top, about 10 minutes. Serve immediately, accompanied by Plums in Lime.

COOK'S FILE

Storage time: Make this dish just before serving.

WHITE AND BLACK TRUFFLES

Preparation time: 30 minutes +
    5 minutes refrigeration
Cooking time: 10 minutes
Makes about 18

80 g white chocolate
30 g butter
1 tablespoon cream
2 teaspoons white Curaçao

¾ cup grated white chocolate
¼ cup grated dark chocolate

➤ CHOP WHITE chocolate roughly.
1 Combine white chocolate, butter, cream and Curaçao in small heatproof bowl. Stand over a pan of simmering water; stir until chocolate and butter have melted and mixture is smooth. Refrigerate until semi-set.
2 Using electric beaters, beat chocolate mixture until light and creamy.
3 Combine white and dark grated

chocolate. Form heaped teaspoons of mixture into balls and roll balls in grated chocolate. Place on a tray and refrigerate until set.

COOK'S FILE

Storage time: Chocolate truffles can be made several days in advance. Store in layers in an airtight container in the refrigerator.
Variation: These chocolates can be made using all dark or all white chocolate if desired.

Crème Brûlée with Plums in Lime (top)
and White and Black Truffles.

ITALIAN FIESTA

ENTRÉE: Penne with Artichoke Hearts

MAIN: Tuscan Chicken

ACCOMPANIMENT: Olive and Rosemary Focaccia

DESSERT: Poached Peaches and Vanilla Fingers

SWEET TREAT: Spiced Fruit and Nut Bars

PENNE WITH ARTICHOKE HEARTS

Preparation time: 10 minutes
Cooking time: 15 minutes
Serves 8

500 g penne
1 tablespoon olive oil
2 leeks, thinly sliced
2 medium red capsicums, cut
    into 1 cm strips
2 garlic cloves, crushed
400 g can artichoke hearts,
    drained and quartered
1 tablespoon lemon juice
30 g butter
40 g fresh parmesan cheese

➤ COOK PASTA in a large pan of boiling water until just tender.
1 Meanwhile, heat oil in a medium heavy-based pan, add leeks and cook, stirring, on medium heat for 3 minutes.

2 Add capsicum and garlic and cook, stirring, for 3 minutes. Stir in artichoke hearts and lemon juice.
3 Drain pasta and return to large pan. Add butter and stir through to coat pasta, then add artichoke mixture and combine well. Serve immediately, with shavings of fresh parmesan.

COOK'S FILE

Storage time: Make this dish just before serving.
Note: Make sure leeks are well washed before slicing.
Variation: Penne is short pasta tubes. If they are not available, you could substitute any other short pasta, such as spirals, shells or bows.
Marinated artichokes can also be used; drain them well.
Wine suggestions: With this Italian menu, Italian wines are perfect. Serve both a chianti and a frascati and let guests help themselves. With dessert, offer a good-quality spumante.

Olive and Rosemary Focaccia (top), Tuscan Chicken and Penne with Artichoke Hearts.

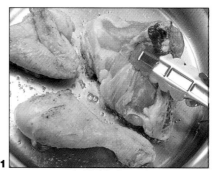

TUSCAN CHICKEN

Preparation time: 20 minutes
Cooking time: 1½ hours
Serves 8

2 x 1.4 kg chickens
¼ cup olive oil
1 cup dry white wine
1½ cups vegetable stock
3 tablespoons tomato paste
2 teaspoons dried sage
1 tablespoon capers
4 spring onions, finely chopped
4 celery sticks, sliced
8 green button squash
2 tablespoons chopped parsley

➤ CUT EACH CHICKEN into eight pieces and trim excess fat.

1 Heat oil in a large heavy-based pan and brown chicken pieces in batches. Place pieces into a large baking tray.

2 Preheat oven to moderate 180°C. Combine wine, stock, tomato paste, sage, capers, spring onions and celery in medium pan. Stir over medium heat until mixture boils. Pour sauce over chicken pieces, cover with aluminium foil and bake for 1 hour.

3 Add squash and parsley to pan. Baste chicken and squash and return pan to oven. Bake, uncovered, for 30 minutes, basting every 10 minutes.

4 Remove chicken and squash to a serving dish. Keep warm. Pour the liquid into a pan. Stir over medium heat until mixture boils; reduce heat and simmer 5 minutes or until reduced by half. Serve chicken with sauce and a green salad.

COOK'S FILE

Storage time: This dish can be cooked one day ahead up to the end of Step 3. Store dish, covered, in the refrigerator. Before serving, reheat gently, then continue as above.

OLIVE AND ROSEMARY FOCACCIA

Preparation time: 30 minutes +
55 minutes proving time
Cooking time: 30 minutes
Makes 8 rolls

7 g sachet dry yeast
1 teaspoon sugar
¾ cup warm water
2¾ cups plain flour
1 teaspoon salt
1 tablespoon dried rosemary
1 tablespoon olive oil
⅓ cup black olives, sliced
2 tablespoons olive oil, extra

➤ COMBINE YEAST and sugar in a small mixing bowl.

1 Gradually add ¼ cup of the warm water; blend until smooth. Stand, covered with plastic wrap, in a warm place for 10 minutes or until foamy.

2 Sift flour and salt into a large mixing bowl. Stir in dried rosemary. Make a well in the centre, add olive oil, yeast mixture and remaining water. Using a knife, mix to a firm dough.

3 Turn dough onto a lightly floured surface, knead for 10 minutes. Shape dough into a ball, place in large, lightly oiled mixing bowl. Leave, covered with plastic wrap, in a warm place for 45 minutes or until well risen.

4 Preheat oven to moderately hot 210°C. Brush two 32 x 28 cm oven trays with oil. Knead dough again for 2 minutes or until smooth. Divide dough into eight pieces. Knead one portion at a time on lightly floured surface for 1 minute and shape into a flat 10 cm round. Repeat with remaining dough. Press sliced olives onto surface of dough, and brush with extra olive oil. Bake 30 minutes or until golden brown. Cool on a wire rack.

COOK'S FILE

Storage time: Olive and Rosemary Focaccia may be made up to six hours ahead. To serve hot, reheat in a warm oven for 5 minutes before serving.

Note: Focaccia is a traditional Italian bread. It can be made in small rounds as here, or in large trays and cut into squares to serve.

Variation: Omit olives and sprinkle focaccia with a little crushed sea salt.

POACHED PEACHES WITH MARSALA CREAM AND VANILLA FINGERS

Preparation time: 50 minutes
Cooking time: 30 minutes
Serves 8

4 egg yolks
¼ cup caster sugar
¼ cup marsala
1¼ cups cream, whipped
1 cup sugar
4 cups water
8 medium peaches

Vanilla Fingers
60 g butter
¾ cup icing sugar
2 egg whites
¼ teaspoon vanilla essence
½ cup plain flour

➤ USING ELECTRIC beaters, beat egg yolks and sugar in a medium heatproof bowl for 1 minute.

1 Place bowl over a pan of simmering water; beat constantly until just warmed through. Add marsala gradually to egg mixture, whisking for about 3 minutes or until thick and foamy. Remove from heat and continue whisking for another 2 minutes or until mixture cools. Transfer to a clean bowl, and fold in whipped cream. Cover and refrigerate until required.

2 Combine sugar and water in a large, heavy-based pan. Stir over medium heat until sugar has completely dissolved. Bring to the boil, reduce heat slightly and add whole peaches. Simmer, covered, for 20 minutes, turning peaches occasionally to ensure even cooking. Using a slotted spoon, lift peaches carefully from syrup onto a plate and allow to cool. Remove skins gently with fingers. Store, covered with plastic wrap, in the refrigerator until needed. Stand peaches at room temperature for 15 minutes before serving.

3 To make Vanilla Fingers: Preheat oven to moderate 180°C. Cut two pieces of baking paper to fit two 32 x 28 cm biscuit trays. Using a pencil and ruler, draw parallel lines 7 cm apart. Brush trays with a little melted butter or oil, and place paper pencil-side down. Using electric beaters, beat butter and icing sugar in a medium mixing bowl until light and creamy. Add egg whites gradually, beating thoroughly after each addition. Add essence; beat until combined. Using a metal spoon, fold in sifted flour.

4 Spoon mixture into a piping bag fitted with a 1 cm plain nozzle. Using drawn lines as a guide, pipe mixture into 7 cm lengths, leaving about 5 cm between each finger. Bake 7 minutes or until just lightly golden. Leave on tray until firm, then lift onto a wire rack to cool completely. To serve, arrange a peach with a large dollop of Marsala Cream and three Vanilla Fingers on each plate.

COOK'S FILE

Storage time: Cook Marsala Cream and peaches up to three hours ahead; store in the refrigerator. Vanilla Fingers may be made up to one day ahead; store in an airtight container.

SPICED FRUIT AND NUT BARS

Preparation time: 20 minutes
Cooking time: 30 minutes
Makes 32

2/3 cup blanched almonds
2/3 cup walnuts
1/2 cup mixed peel
1/3 cup mixed dried fruit
2 tablespoons cocoa
2 tablespoons plain flour
1/2 teaspoon ground cinnamon
1/4 teaspoon ground cloves
1/4 teaspoon ground nutmeg
1/3 cup caster sugar
1/4 cup honey
1/4 cup water
250 g dark compound
    chocolate, chopped

➤ PREHEAT OVEN to moderate 180°C. Line a 20 cm square cake tin with aluminium foil, brush foil with melted butter or oil.

1 Spread almonds and walnuts on an oven tray and bake for 5 minutes or until just golden. Remove from tray to cool and chop finely. Combine nuts, peel, dried fruit, cocoa, flour and spices in a large mixing bowl.
2 Combine sugar, honey and water in a small heavy-based pan. Stir over medium heat without boiling until sugar has completely dissolved. Brush sugar crystals from sides of pan with a wet brush. Bring to the boil, reduce heat slightly, boil for 10 minutes without stirring. Remove from heat, pour onto fruit mixture and, using a wooden spoon, combine well.
3 Press into prepared tin with the back of an oiled spoon and bake for 20 minutes. Cool in tin. Remove cake from tin and peel away foil. Using a long sharp knife, cut crusts from edges and discard. Cut cake into four long bars, then each bar into eight short fingers.
4 Line a large oven tray with aluminium foil. Place chocolate in a small heatproof bowl. Stand over a pan of simmering water, stir until chocolate has melted and mixture is smooth. Cool slightly. Dip each fruit bar into melted chocolate. Using a spoon, carefully coat in chocolate and then lift out on a fork. Drain excess chocolate, then place onto prepared tray. Allow to set.

COOK'S FILE

Storage time: This dish can be made up to one week ahead. Store in an airtight container in a cool, dark place.

SPRING GATHERING

ENTRÉE:	Asparagus with Orange Hollandaise
MAIN:	Lamb Loin with Roast Garlic
ACCOMPANIMENT:	Mediterranean-style Vegetables
DESSERT:	Individual Strawberry Meringues
SWEET TREAT:	Grand Marnier Truffles

ASPARAGUS WITH ORANGE HOLLANDAISE

Preparation time: 30 minutes
Cooking time: 20 minutes
Serves 6

1 sheet ready-rolled puff pastry
175 g unsalted butter
2 tablespoons water
4 egg yolks
2 tablespoons orange juice
salt and white pepper, to taste
24 asparagus spears, trimmed

➤ PREHEAT OVEN to moderate 180˚C.
1 Brush a 32 x 28 cm oven tray with melted butter or oil. Cut pastry into six rectangles, place on tray and bake 15 minutes or until puffed and golden. Set aside to cool.
2 Melt butter in a small pan. Skim froth from top and discard. Allow melted butter to cool but not re-set. Combine water and egg yolks in a small pan; whisk 30 seconds or until pale and creamy. Place pan over low heat and continue whisking for 3 minutes, until mixture is thick. Remove from heat and add cooled butter a little at a time, whisking between each addition. (Leave whey in the bottom of the pan.) Stir in juice, season to taste. Transfer sauce to a jug; keep at room temperature.
3 Place asparagus in a medium pan with a little boiling water. Cook over low heat until just tender; drain.
To serve, carefully split pastry rectangles in half. Place bottom pieces of pastry on each plate, lay four spears of asparagus across, drizzle with Orange Hollandaise, and top with pastry cap.

COOK'S FILE

Storage time: Pastry may be cooked up to 12 hours in advance. Store in an airtight container.

Asparagus with Orange Hollandaise (left) and Lamb Loin with Roast Garlic.

LAMB LOIN WITH ROAST GARLIC

Preparation time: 30 minutes
Cooking time: 45 minutes
Serves 6

2 x 500 g boned loins of lamb
6 English spinach leaves
2 tablespoons pine nuts
2 teaspoons fresh rosemary, finely chopped
1 tablespoon olive oil
1/4 teaspoon cracked black pepper
18 cloves garlic, unpeeled
1 tablespoon olive oil, extra
6 sprigs fresh rosemary
1/2 cup red wine
1/2 cup vegetable stock

➤ PREHEAT OVEN to moderate 180°C. Trim excess fat and sinew from meat, lay out flat.

1 Wash spinach leaves and shake off excess water, leaving slightly damp. Shred finely and place in a small pan over low heat, stirring until spinach is just limp. Remove from heat, drain and combine in a small mixing bowl with pine nuts and chopped rosemary.

2 Divide spinach mixture in two; place across centre of each loin. Roll and tie up meat securely with string at regular intervals to retain its shape. Heat oil in a deep baking dish on top of stove; add meat and brown all over on high heat. Sprinkle with black pepper. Brush garlic cloves with extra oil and place with rosemary sprigs around meat in baking dish. Place dish in oven and bake for 45 minutes.

3 Remove meat and garlic cloves from baking dish and place on a heated plate to keep warm. Place dish on top of stove, add red wine and stock and stir over medium heat until mixture boils. Reduce heat slightly and simmer for 5 minutes or until reduced by half. Strain into a small jug.

To serve, slice each loin into nine pieces and place three pieces on each plate with whole garlic cloves. Pour over a little red wine sauce.

COOK'S FILE

Storage time: Cook this dish just before serving.

Hint: Do not be frightened by the amount of garlic in this recipe. Roasting garlic mellows the flavour and it becomes very mild and sweet. Each diner squeezes the garlic cloves to extract the garlic. Warm plates to keep food hot when serving.

1

2

3

4

MEDITERRANEAN-STYLE VEGETABLES

Preparation time: 30 minutes +
  1 hour standing
Cooking time: 15 minutes
Serves 6

1 large eggplant
1 tablespoon salt
250 g punnet cherry tomatoes
1 medium red capsicum, halved
1 tablespoon olive oil
1 small green capsicum, cut
  into 2 cm squares
2 medium zucchini, sliced
90 g button mushrooms, halved
⅓ cup fresh basil leaves
2 tablespoons chopped fresh
  oregano leaves
2 tablespoons balsamic vinegar
1 tablespoon olive oil, extra

➤ PREHEAT OVEN to moderate 180°C. Brush an oven tray with oil.
1 Cut eggplant lengthways into thin slices, spread out in a single layer on a board; sprinkle with salt. Set aside for 15 minutes; rinse and dry thoroughly. Place eggplant slices in a single layer on tray.
2 Score a small cross in each tomato, place on tray with eggplant. Brush eggplant and tomatoes with oil; bake for 10 minutes. Remove from oven and allow to cool. Cut eggplant into strips.
3 Remove seeds from red capsicum; brush skin with oil. Grill until skin is black, then wrap in a damp tea-towel until cool. Rub off skin, and slice. Place zucchini in a small heatproof bowl. Cover with boiling water, stand for 1 minute, drain and plunge into cold water, drain well. Shred basil leaves.
4 Combine all vegetables and herbs in a large mixing bowl. Sprinkle vinegar and oil over, and toss well to combine. Allow to stand for 1 hour for flavours to combine, then serve at room temperature. Serve with Lamb Loin.

COOK'S FILE

Storage time: Make this dish one hour before serving.
Wine suggestions: Serve sauvignon blanc with the entrée and a medium cabernet sauvignon with the Lamb Loin with Roast Garlic.

INDIVIDUAL STRAWBERRY MERINGUES

Preparation time: 25 minutes
Cooking time: 40 minutes
Serves 6

4 egg whites
1 cup caster sugar
2 x 250g punnets strawberries, hulled
1¼ cups cream, whipped

➤ PREHEAT OVEN to slow 150°C. Brush two 32 x 28 cm oven trays with melted butter or oil. Cut non-stick baking paper to fit trays.

1 Using an 8 cm-round cutter as a guide, mark 12 circles onto paper, and place pencil-side down on trays.
2 Place egg whites in a medium, clean dry mixing bowl. Using electric beaters, beat until soft peaks form. Add sugar gradually, beating constantly until mixture is thick and glossy and all the sugar has dissolved. Spread meringue into rounds on prepared tray. Bake 40 minutes then turn off heat and allow to cool in oven.
3 Place 1 punnet of strawberries into food processor or blender and blend until completely liquid. Slice remaining strawberries and fold through whipped cream.
To serve, sandwich two meringue rounds together with cream mixture and place on each plate. Pour strawberry sauce around base of meringue.

COOK'S FILE

Storage time: Meringues may be made up to two days in advance. Store in an airtight container. Strawberry sauce may be made up to one day ahead. Make strawberry cream mixture up to two hours in advance. Store sauce and cream, covered, in the refrigerator. Once dessert is assembled, serve immediately.
Variation: For a sweeter sauce, add a little caster sugar. Garnish dish with strawberry leaves to serve, if liked.
Wine suggestion: Sweet champagne, sauternes or a botrytised semillon would go well with this dessert.

GRAND MARNIER TRUFFLES

Preparation time: 20 minutes + 1 hour refrigeration
Cooking time: 5 minutes
Makes 24

225 g dark chocolate, chopped
45 g butter
⅓ cup cream
1 tablespoon Grand Marnier
80 g dark chocolate, extra, finely grated

➤ PLACE CHOCOLATE in a medium mixing bowl.
1 Combine butter and cream in a small, heavy-based pan; stir over low heat until butter has melted. Bring to the boil, then remove from heat.
2 Pour hot cream mixture over chocolate. Using a wooden spoon, stir until chocolate has melted and mixture is smooth. Stir in Grand Marnier.
3 Cool in the refrigerator, stirring occasionally. When mixture is firm enough to handle, roll heaped teaspoons into balls. Place grated chocolate into small mixing bowl. Roll each truffle in chocolate until completely coated. Refrigerate until firm. Serve with coffee and a glass of Grand Marnier or your favourite liqueur.

COOK'S FILE

Storage time: Truffles may be made up to three days in advance and stored in an airtight container in the refrigerator. Allow truffles to stand at room temperature for 10 minutes before serving.
Hint: To avoid finger marks on truffles, re-roll in grated chocolate just before serving.

Individual Strawberry Meringues (top) and Grand Marnier Truffles.

SUMMER FESTIVAL

APPETISER: Tomato and Olive Crispbread

ENTRÉE: Smoked Salmon and Dill Crêpes

MAIN: Coriander Chilli Prawns

ACCOMPANIMENT: Orange Sesame Rice Salad

DESSERT: Summer Fruit Compote

TOMATO AND OLIVE CRISPBREAD

Preparation time: 20 minutes
Cooking time: 20 minutes
Serves 8

2 large onions, sliced in rings
20 g butter
2 teaspoons olive oil
⅓ cup pimiento-stuffed olives
⅓ cup sun-dried tomatoes, drained
2 sheets lavash bread

➤ PREHEAT OVEN to moderate 180°C. Line two 32 x 28 cm oven trays with aluminium foil.

1 Heat butter and oil in a medium heavy-based frypan. Add onion, cook over medium-high heat until dark golden brown. Remove from heat. Drain on absorbent paper.

2 Place olives and tomatoes in food processor bowl. Using the pulse action, press button for 20 seconds or until mixture is fairly smooth. Spread mixture evenly over bread. Top with onion rings, place on prepared trays. Bake 20 minutes or until dark and crisp.

3 Leave to stand 5 minutes before removing from trays. Cut into squares or triangles to serve.

COOK'S FILE

Storage time: Cook this dish just before serving.

Note: Lavash bread is very thin, unleavened bread, available from delicatessens and some supermarkets.

Variation: Substitute black olives for stuffed and add anchovies to the mixture before processing, if desired. If lavash is unavailable, Lebanese or pita bread can be used.

Wine suggestions: A mature semillon or a mature fumé blanc could be drunk throughout this meal. A light pinot noir or rosé would also suit.

Smoked Salmon and Dill Crêpes (top) and Tomato and Olive Crispbread.

SMOKED SALMON AND DILL CRÊPES

Preparation time: 50 minutes
Cooking time: 25 minutes
Makes 9 crêpes

Crêpes
1 cup plain flour
1 egg, lightly beaten
1½ cups milk

Filling
150 g cream cheese, softened
1 tablespoon sour cream
1 tablespoon chopped dill
2 teaspoons chopped mint
1 tablespoon lemon juice
1 small avocado, mashed
200 g smoked salmon, thinly
   sliced
sprigs of dill, for garnish

➤ Sift flour into a medium mixing bowl; make a well in the centre.

1 Using a wooden spoon, gradually stir in combined egg and milk. Beat until all liquid is incorporated and batter is free of lumps. Transfer mixture to jug; cover with plastic wrap and leave for 30 minutes.

2 To make Filling: Using electric beaters, beat cream cheese in small mixing bowl until creamy. Add sour cream, dill, mint, juice and avocado, beat 30 seconds or until mixture is smooth and creamy. Cover with plastic wrap, refrigerate until needed.

3 Pour 2-3 tablespoons batter onto lightly greased 20 cm crêpe pan, swirl evenly over base. Cook over medium heat 1 minute or until underside is golden. Turn crêpe over; cook other side. Transfer to a plate; cover with tea-towel, keep warm. Repeat process with remaining batter, greasing pan when necessary.

4 Spread each crêpe evenly with filling, top with salmon slices. Stack crêpes on top of each other. Using a sharp knife, cut into eight wedges. Garnish with dill sprigs. Serve with a green salad.

COOK'S FILE

Storage time: Batter can be made one day ahead. Store, covered, in the refrigerator. Cook crêpes and assemble dish just before serving.

CORIANDER CHILLI PRAWNS

Preparation time: 20 minutes + 1 hour
 marinating
Cooking time: 10 minutes
Serves 8

48 medium green king prawns
1/3 cup finely chopped fresh
 coriander
2 tablespoons oil
1/4 cup soy sauce
1/4 cup sweet chilli sauce
1 tablespoon sweet soy sauce

2 tablespoons plum sauce
zest of 2 limes
1/4 cup lime juice

➤ DISCARD ANY prawns with broken shells.

1 Using a sharp knife, cut down the back of each prawn and remove the vein, leaving the shell intact.

2 Combine remaining ingredients in large mixing bowl, stir until well combined. Add prawns, mix well. Cover with plastic wrap, refrigerate 1 hour. Drain and reserve marinade.

3 Place prawns on lightly oiled grill or flat plate. Grill under high heat, turning regularly, for 10 minutes or until shells are pink and crisp and flesh is white. Baste with marinade while cooking.

COOK'S FILE

Storage time: Prawns can be marinated for up to four hours.
Variation: Prawns can be cooked by stir-frying. Heat 1 tablespoon oil in wok or heavy-based frypan and cook prawns in small batches over high heat until shells are pink and crisp and flesh is white. Serve immediately.
Hint: Offer finger bowls for each diner with this dish.

1

2

3

ORANGE SESAME RICE SALAD

Preparation time: 40 minutes
Cooking time: 15 minutes
Serves 8

12 fresh asparagus spears
2 cups long-grain rice, cooked and cooled
1 Lebanese cucumber, thinly sliced
150 g small snow peas
1 large red capsicum, thinly sliced
2 large spring onions
1 Spanish onion, thinly sliced
2 oranges

Dressing
2 tablespoons sesame oil
2/3 cup orange juice
2 teaspoons grated ginger
2 teaspoons finely grated orange rind
1 clove garlic, crushed
1 tablespoon honey

➤ PLUNGE ASPARAGUS spears into bowl of boiling water. Leave 2 minutes, until vibrant green in colour and slightly tender. Drain, then plunge into bowl of ice water. When cold, drain; pat dry with absorbent paper.
1 Cut asparagus into 3 cm pieces diagonally. Top and tail snow peas.
2 Place oranges on a board. Cut a slice off the end of each orange, to where the flesh starts. Cut the skin away in a circular motion, cutting only deep enough to remove all the white membrane. Separate segments by cutting between membrane and flesh. Do this over a bowl to catch any juice.
3 Combine all ingredients in a large mixing bowl. Pour Dressing over and stir until well combined. Transfer salad to serving bowl. Serve with Coriander Chilli Prawns.
4 To make Dressing: Place all ingredients in a small jar. Shake vigorously for 30 seconds or until well combined.

COOK'S FILE

Storage time: This salad can be made several hours in advance.
Note: Sesame oil is available from Asian food stores.

SUMMER FRUIT COMPOTE

Preparation time: 40 minutes
Cooking time: 30 minutes
Serves 8

5 apricots, halved and stoned
4 nectarines, halved and stoned
4 blood plums, stoned
4 peaches, stoned and cut in
    quarters
200 g cherries, stoned
1 cup good-quality claret
⅓ cup dry sherry
1 cup water
¾ cup caster sugar

➤ GENTLY PLUNGE FRUIT in small batches into a bowl of boiling water for 1 minute.

1 Remove with a slotted spoon. Carefully remove skins from fruit except for cherries. Set aside in a bowl of ice water.

2 Combine claret, sherry, water and sugar in large heavy-based pan. Stir over low heat without boiling until sugar has dissolved. Bring to boil, reduce heat and simmer 5 minutes.

3 Add fruits to syrup in small batches and simmer each batch for 5 minutes. Remove with a slotted spoon. Pile fruits onto serving plate or bowl. Bring syrup to the boil, reduce heat, simmer for further 5 minutes. Remove from heat, cool slightly. Pour syrup over fruits. Serve with a dollop of freshly whipped cream.

COOK'S FILE

Storage time: This dish can be served hot or cold. Store, covered, in refrigerator for up to one day.

AUTUMN BOUNTY

APPETISER: Poppy Seed Twists

ENTRÉE: Apple and Blue Cheese Soup

MAIN: Pork with Soy-orange Sauce

ACCOMPANIMENT: Parsnip Chips

DESSERT: Individual Butter Puddings with Golden Syrup Cream

POPPY SEED TWISTS

Preparation time: 20 minutes
Cooking time: 15 minutes +
   15 minutes refrigeration
Makes 24

½ cup plain flour
35 g butter, chopped
2 tablespoons iced water
1 tablespoon poppy seeds
1 egg, beaten

➤ PREHEAT OVEN to moderate 180°C. Brush a 32 x 28 cm oven tray with melted butter or oil.

1 Place flour in a medium mixing bowl, make a well in the centre and add butter. Using two knives, cut butter in a crossing motion until reduced to very small pieces. Stir in the water with a knife and mix to a firm dough. Turn out onto a lightly floured surface, knead 1 minute or until smooth. Store, covered in plastic wrap, in refrigerator for 15 minutes.

2 On a lightly floured surface, roll pastry to a 24 x 16 cm rectangle. Sprinkle with poppy seeds; press them gently into the pastry with the back of a spoon. Fold pastry into three layers, and re-roll to a 30 x 12 cm rectangle. Cut crossways into 24 strips.

3 Hold a strip at each end, and twist ends in opposite directions. Place on prepared tray and brush lightly with beaten egg. Bake for 15 minutes or until golden. Cool on a wire rack. Serve as an appetiser or with Apple and Blue Cheese Soup.

COOK'S FILE

Storage time: Poppy Seed Twists can be made up to two days ahead and stored in an airtight container.
Wine suggestions: With this dish, serve a riesling or young chardonnay.

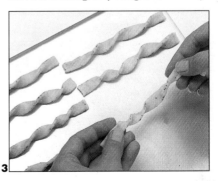

Apple and Blue Cheese Soup (top) and Poppy Seed Twists.

APPLE AND BLUE CHEESE SOUP

Preparation time: 20 minutes
Cooking time: 30 minutes
Serves 8

40 g butter
2 tablespoons plain flour
3 cups chicken stock
4 medium red apples
2 cups milk
250 g blue cheese

➤ MELT BUTTER in a large heavy-based pan.

1 Add flour to pan. Stir over low heat for 2 minutes or until flour mixture is lightly golden. Add stock gradually to pan, stirring until mixture is smooth.

2 Peel, core and slice apples and add to stock mixture. Cook, covered, over medium heat 20 minutes or until tender. Cool and purée mixture in batches until smooth. Return to pan.

3 Add milk and reheat soup; stirring. Simmer gently, and add crumbled cheese. Stir well until mixture is smooth and serve immediately with Poppy Seed Twists.

COOK'S FILE

Storage time: Soup can be made up to Step 3 one day in advance and stored, covered, in the refrigerator. Complete recipe just before serving.
Hint: Varieties of blue cheese suitable for use in this recipe include stilton, Danish blue and roquefort.
Variation: If blue cheese is not to your taste, substitute a plain creamy cheese, such as camembert or brie.

PORK WITH SOY-ORANGE SAUCE

Preparation time: 10 minutes +
  overnight marinating
Cooking time: 10 minutes each batch
Serves 8

8 (about 180 g each) pork
  butterfly medallions
  or pork chops
3/4 cup orange juice
1/4 cup soy sauce
2 tablespoons olive oil
2 cloves garlic, crushed
2 teaspoons dried rosemary
1 tablespoon honey
1 tablespoon olive oil, extra,
  for frying

➤ TRIM MEAT of excess fat and sinew. Place pork steaks in a single layer in a large, shallow glass or ceramic dish.

1 Combine orange juice, soy sauce, oil, garlic, rosemary and honey and pour over steaks. Place in refrigerator to marinate for 8 hours, or overnight.

2 Preheat oven to slow 150°C. Heat oil in a large, heavy-based pan; remove steaks from marinade, reserving marinade. Add steaks to pan. (Unless you have a very big pan, you will have to cook them in batches.) Cook over medium heat 4-5 minutes each side. Remove from heat and drain on absorbent paper. Place cooked steaks on a plate and cover loosely with foil. Keep warm in oven while you cook remaining steaks.

3 Pour marinade into pan. Stir over medium heat until mixture boils; reduce heat slightly and simmer for about 5 minutes or until reduced by half. To serve, place a steak on each plate and spoon over a little of the sauce. Accompany with a steamed green vegetable such as asparagus or snow peas.

COOK'S FILE

Storage time: This dish can be marinated a day ahead up to the end of Step 1. Complete just before serving.
Wine suggestions: The strong flavours in this main course call for a similarly full-bodied cabernet sauvignon or shiraz, or try a more subtle pinot noir. Pork also marries very well with sparkling burgundy.

Apple and Blue Cheese Soup (top) and Pork with Soy-orange Sauce.

PARSNIP CHIPS

Preparation time: 10 minutes
Cooking time: 6 minutes
Serves 8

**4 large parsnips
2 tablespoons lemon juice
oil for deep frying**

➤ PEEL PARSNIPS.
1 Cut parsnips diagonally into 3 mm slices. Place slices in a large bowl and cover with water. Add lemon juice to water. Set aside.
2 When ready to cook, drain parsnip slices and thoroughly dry with absorbent paper.
3 Heat oil in deep heavy-based pan. Gently lower one-third of the parsnip slices into moderately hot oil. Cook over medium-high heat for 1-2 minutes or until golden, remove with tongs. Repeat with remaining parsnip slices. Drain chips on absorbent paper and serve immediately.

COOK'S FILE

Storage time: Parsnip slices can remain in the water and lemon juice, in the refrigerator, for up to two hours before cooking.
Variation: Parsnips are also delicious as a side dish, steamed or boiled and mashed with a generous amount of butter and freshly ground black pepper. Choose young parsnips. For steaming, cut into even-size pieces. For boiling, put chopped parsnips into cold water and gently simmer until soft.
Hint: For best results when deep-frying, use peanut, corn, safflower or soybean oil. These oils have a bland flavour and a high smoking point, which means that they can be heated to a very high temperature without burning or smoking.

INDIVIDUAL BUTTER PUDDINGS WITH GOLDEN SYRUP CREAM

Preparation time: 20 minutes
Cooking time: 25 minutes
Serves 8

125 g butter
¾ cup caster sugar
2 eggs, lightly beaten
1 teaspoon vanilla
   essence
1½ cups self-raising flour
½ cup milk

Golden Syrup Cream
60 g butter, extra
½ cup golden syrup
1¼ cups cream

➤ PREHEAT OVEN to moderate 180°C. Brush eight 1-cup capacity ovenproof ramekins or moulds with melted butter.

1 Using electric beaters, beat butter and sugar in a small mixing bowl until light and creamy. Add eggs gradually, beating thoroughly after each addition. Add essence; beat until combined. Transfer mixture to a large mixing bowl. Using a metal spoon, fold in sifted flour alternately with milk. Stir until just combined and mixture is almost smooth.

2 Spoon mixture into prepared tins; place on a large oven tray, and bake for 20 minutes or until a skewer comes out clean when inserted in centre of pudding. Leave the puddings in tins for 5 minutes before turning out onto a wire rack to cool.

3 To make Golden Syrup Cream: Melt butter in a small heavy-based pan. Add golden syrup and stir over medium heat until well combined. Add cream and bring to the boil, stirring constantly. Transfer to a jug. To serve, place a pudding on each plate and drizzle with Golden Syrup Cream. Serve with cream or vanilla ice-cream.

COOK'S FILE

Storage time: Puddings can be made up to two hours in advance. Store at room temperature, covered with a clean tea-towel. Make Golden Syrup Cream just before serving.
Variation: Add ½ cup chopped fresh dates or raisins to the butter mixture.
Wine suggestions: Try a sweet dessert-style sauternes or botrytised semillon with this dish.

WINTER WELCOME

ENTRÉE: Vegetable Timbales with Tomato Sauce

MAIN: Roast Lamb with Sage and Tarragon

ACCOMPANIMENT: Peppery Sprouts and Baby Squash

DESSERT: Caramel Soufflé Gateau

VEGETABLE TIMBALES WITH TOMATO SAUCE

Preparation time: 1 hour
Cooking time: 20 minutes
Serves 6

1 cup Arborio rice, cooked
1 tablespoon olive oil
1 small red capsicum
100 g button mushrooms
1 clove garlic, crushed
3 spring onions, finely
  chopped
50 g cheddar cheese, grated
2 tablespoons grated parmesan
  cheese
cracked black pepper
15 g butter

Tomato Sauce
2 teaspoons olive oil
3 large ripe tomatoes,
  finely chopped
2 tablespoons tomato paste
2 teaspoons balsamic vinegar

▶ LIGHTLY GREASE six ½-cup capacity timbale moulds with oil.

1 Finely chop capsicum and mushrooms. Heat oil in a large, heavy-based pan. Add garlic, capsicum, mushrooms and onions. Stir over medium heat for 2–3 minutes or until softened. Stir in hot rice, cheeses, pepper to taste and butter. Stir until cheese melts.

2 Spoon mixture into prepared moulds, pack in tightly, to give timbales shape. (No further cooking is necessary.) Place a knife down the side of each mould; carefully ease timbales out; cover with foil. Keep warm.

3 To make Sauce: Heat oil in medium, heavy-based pan. Add tomato and paste. Stir over medium heat 3 minutes or until tomato is very soft. Stir in vinegar. Place timbales on serving plates; spoon sauce around.

COOK'S FILE

Storage time: Timbales can be assembled 3 hours ahead. Reheat gently.
Hint: Arborio rice is high-quality Italian rice, available from delicatessens.

Peppery Sprouts and Baby Squash (top right), Caramel Soufflé Gateau and Vegetable Timbales with Tomato Sauce.

ROAST LAMB WITH SAGE AND TARRAGON

Preparation time: 15 minutes
Cooking time: 1 hour 15 minutes
Serves 6

2 kg leg of lamb
1/4 cup roughly chopped fresh
  sage leaves
2 tablespoons roughly chopped
  fresh tarragon leaves
1 clove garlic
1 medium onion, chopped
1 tablespoon oil
2 tablespoons plum sauce
1 cup white wine
1/4 cup chicken stock

➤ PREHEAT OVEN to moderate 180°C. Using a small, sharp knive, trim meat of excess fat and sinew.

1 Combine sage, tarragon, garlic, onion, oil and plum sauce in food processor bowl. Using the pulse action, process for 30 seconds or until mixture is smooth.

2 Place meat in a deep baking dish. Rub meat all over with sage mixture. Add a little water to base of dish to prevent burning. Bake, uncovered, for 1 hour 15 minutes. Remove from oven, place on carving platter. Cover loosely with foil and leave in a warm place for 10 minutes before slicing.

3 Place baking dish on top of stove. Add wine and stock to pan juices, stirring well to incorporate browned bits

off the bottom of the pan. Bring to boil, reduce heat, simmer 5 minutes. Pour over lamb to serve. Serve with Peppery Sprouts and Baby Squash.

COOK'S FILE

Storage time: Cook this dish just before serving.

Wine suggestions: With this menu you could serve a chardonnay with the first course, a cabernet sauvignon with the Roast Lamb and a sweet dessert wine with the Gateau. Or, drink cabernet sauvignon or claret throughout the meal but not with dessert, as the sweet creaminess of the cake would be overwhelmed by the strong-flavoured wine. Some people find champagne a pleasant way to finish a special meal.

PEPPERY SPROUTS AND BABY SQUASH

Preparation time: 15 minutes
Cooking time: 10 minutes
Serves 6

2 rashers bacon
12 small Brussels sprouts
12 small yellow or green
  baby squash
1 tablespoon pine nuts
1 teaspoon cracked black
  pepper

➤ REMOVE RIND from bacon.

1 Cut bacon into thin strips. Trim any rough outer leaves from Brussels sprouts and cut in half lengthways.

2 Cook bacon in a medium, heavy-based pan until browned. Stir in sprouts and squash, cook 2 minutes. Cover tightly and cook over medium heat for 5–10 minutes or until vegetables are just tender.

3 Add pine nuts and pepper to pan; mix gently to combine. Cover pan and cook a further 30–40 seconds. Remove from heat. Serve immediately with Roast Lamb.

COOK'S FILE

Storage time: Cook this dish just before serving.

Variation: If fresh Brussels sprouts are unavailable, frozen ones can be used. Three medium zucchini, sliced, can also be used to replace either of the vegetables in this recipe.

Hint: Be careful not to overcook vegetables. For best taste, texture and nutritional value, cook vegetables until they are just tender. Never add soda to green vegetables, as this depletes their vitamin content.

Peppery Sprouts and Baby Squash (top) and
Roast Lamb with Sage and Tarragon

CARAMEL SOUFFLÉ GATEAU

Preparation time: 1 hour + 30 minutes
+ overnight refrigeration
Cooking time: 35 minutes
Makes one 20 cm round cake

150 g butter
⅔ cup caster sugar
1 tablespoon raw sugar
1 tablespoon glucose syrup
2 eggs, lightly beaten
2 teaspoons vanilla essence
1½ cups self-raising flour
½ cup buttermilk
2 tablespoons cocoa powder, sifted
825 g can pear slices, drained; juice reserved

Mousse
50 g butter
¼ cup brown sugar
½ cup reserved pear juice
2 tablespoons golden syrup
2 teaspoons gelatine
2 eggs, separated
2 cups cream, whipped to firm peaks

➤ PREHEAT OVEN to moderate 180°C. Brush a deep, 17 cm round tin and a deep, 23 cm square tin with melted butter or oil. Line bases and sides with paper; grease paper.

1 Using electric beaters, beat butter, sugars and glucose in small mixing bowl until light and creamy. Add eggs gradually, beating thoroughly after each addition. Add essence; beat until combined. Transfer mixture to large mixing bowl. Using a metal spoon, fold in sifted flour alternately with buttermilk. Stir until just combined and the mixture is smooth.

2 Spoon half the mixture into the round tin; smooth surface. Spoon half the remaining mixture over half of the square tin base. Combine remaining mixture with cocoa; stir until smooth. Spread evenly over the remaining half of the square tin. Bake the round cake for 30 minutes and the square cake for 20 minutes or until a skewer comes out clean when inserted in centre of cakes. Leave cakes in tins 10 minutes before turning onto wire racks to cool.

3 To make Mousse: Combine butter, sugar, pear juice and syrup in medium, heavy-based pan. Stir over low heat without boiling until sugar has completely dissolved. Sprinkle over gelatine, stir until dissolved. Remove from heat; cool slightly. Whisk in egg yolks.

4 Transfer mixture to large mixing bowl. Place egg whites in small, clean, dry mixing bowl. Using electric beaters, beat egg whites until stiff peaks form. Using a metal spoon, gradually fold egg whites and cream into butter mixture. Set aside.

5 Line a deep, 20 cm springform tin with foil, leaving an extra 2 cm at the top. Trim the edges of the square cake. Cut the chocolate half and the vanilla half into 27 even squares each. Place alternate colours in two rows around the inside of the lined tin and press against the side. Carefully place the round cake in the centre, gently easing it into the base.

6 Lay the pear slices overlapping each other on top of the cake base. Top with the mousse mixture. Cover and refrigerate overnight. Cut into wedges to serve.

COOK'S FILE

Storage time: Cook and assemble this dish one day before serving.
Hint: Decorate cake as desired with whipped cream and a few pear slices or chocolate leaves.

4

5

6

SEAFOOD CELEBRATION

APPETISER: Honey Basil Prawns

ENTRÉE: Soufflé Oysters and Oysters with Pine Nuts and Bacon

MAIN: Salmon Cutlets with Vanilla Glaze

ACCOMPANIMENT: Potato Cake

DESSERT: Chocolate and Mascarpone Torte

HONEY BASIL PRAWNS

Preparation time: 20 minutes
Cooking time: 5 minutes +
 30 minutes refrigeration
Serves 6

12 medium green king prawns
2 tablespoons finely chopped
 fresh basil
2 teaspoons honey
1 tablespoon soy sauce
1 teaspoon rice vinegar

➤ PEEL PRAWNS, leaving tail intact.
1 Using a sharp knife, cut down the back of each prawn; remove the vein. Whisk remaining ingredients in a small bowl for 2 minutes or until well combined. Transfer marinade to large bowl; add prawns and mix well to ensure they are covered. Cover with plastic wrap, refrigerate for 30 minutes.

2 Thread one prawn onto each skewer. Cover the ends of skewers with foil to prevent burning.
3 Place prawns on a cold, lightly oiled grill tray, cook prawns under medium-high heat for 2-3 minutes each side or until pink. Remove, serve immediately.

COOK'S FILE

Storage time: Make this dish just before serving.
Variation: Fresh scallops are a good alternative to prawns.
Hint: To prevent burning, soak bamboo skewers in water for a few hours.
Wine suggestions: Sauvignon blanc is the first choice for this menu; however, a crisp young semillon or chardonnay would also marry well. In summer, serve an icy beer or glass of champagne (depending on the occasion) with the appetiser. Try an aged, sweet Rhine riesling or a liqueur muscat with the dessert torte.

Salmon Cutlets with Vanilla Glaze (top) and Honey Basil Prawns.

SOUFFLÉ OYSTERS

Preparation time: 25 minutes
Cooking time: 20 minutes
Serves 6

18 oysters in the shell
25 g butter
1 tablespoon self-raising flour
½ cup milk
2 teaspoons seed mustard
1 egg, separated

➤ PREHEAT OVEN to moderate 180°C. Line a 32 x 28 cm oven tray with foil. Place oysters on tray and remove any grit from oyster surface.

1 Heat butter in a small heavy-based pan; add flour. Stir over low heat 2 minutes or until mixture is lightly golden. Add milk gradually, stirring until mixture is smooth. Stir constantly over medium heat 5 minutes or until mixture boils and thickens. Boil for 1 minute; remove from heat. Cool. Stir in mustard and yolk. Transfer to bowl.

2 Place egg white in a small, clean dry bowl. Using electric beaters, beat until firm peaks form. Using a metal spoon, fold gently into mixture. Spoon heaped teaspoons onto each oyster; bake 15 minutes or until slightly puffed and golden. Serve immediately.

1

2

OYSTERS WITH PINE NUTS AND BACON

Preparation time: 25 minutes
Cooking time: 20 minutes
Serves 6

18 oysters in the shell
2 rashers bacon
2 tablespoons pine nuts, roughly chopped
3 teaspoons Worcestershire sauce
1 tablespoon finely chopped fresh chives

➤ PREHEAT OVEN to moderate 180°C. Line a 32 x 28 cm oven tray with foil. Place oysters on tray. Remove any grit from the surface of oyster flesh.

1 Cook bacon in a small heavy-based pan over medium heat until browned. Add pine nuts and sauce, stir until well combined. Remove from heat.

2 Spoon mixture evenly onto each oyster. Sprinkle with chives. Bake 5-10 minutes or until heated through. Serve immediately with Soufflé Oysters.

COOK'S FILE

Storage time: Assemble oysters several hours in advance; store in refrigerator. Bake just prior to serving.
Wine suggestions: Try stout, champagne or a dry white with oysters.

1

2

Soufflé Oysters (left) and Oysters with Pine Nuts and Bacon.

SALMON CUTLETS WITH VANILLA GLAZE

Preparation time: 40 minutes
Cooking time: 30 minutes
Serves 6

6 (about 200 g) salmon cutlets
¼ cup lemon juice
2 tablespoons water
50 g butter, chopped
2 tablespoons finely chopped
   fresh chives

Vanilla Glaze
1 cup white wine vinegar
¼ cup water
1 vanilla bean
1 tablespoon brown sugar
2 tablespoon sugar
1 teaspoon grated lemon rind

➤ PREHEAT OVEN to moderate 180°C. Remove any scales from fish.
1 Place salmon cutlets in one layer in a large baking dish. Pour over combined lemon juice and water; top with chopped butter.
2 Cover with foil; bake 20 minutes or until fish can be easily flaked with a fork. Place on serving plates, sprinkle on chives and spoon on glaze. Serve immediately with Onion Potato Cake.

3 To make Vanilla Glaze: Combine all ingredients in medium heavy-based pan. Stir over low heat without boiling until sugar has dissolved. Bring to boil, reduce heat, simmer for 5 minutes or until glaze has reduced by half. Remove from heat. Discard vanilla bean.

COOK'S FILE

Storage time: Cook this dish just before serving.
Note: Vanilla beans are available from health food shops or delicatessens. If salmon cutlets are unavailable, use rainbow trout fillets or your favourite fish.

ONION POTATO CAKE

Preparation time: 40 minutes
Cooking time: 50 minutes
Makes one 17 cm round cake

4 large potatoes
1 large Spanish onion
100 g butter, melted
2 cloves garlic, crushed
2 egg yolks
½ cup fine, dry breadcrumbs
¾ cup grated parmesan cheese
cracked black pepper
   to taste

➤ PREHEAT OVEN to moderate 180°C. Line a deep, 17 cm round springform tin with melted butter or oil. Line base and sides with paper; grease paper.
1 Using a sharp knife, cut potatoes and onion into very thin slices.
2 Combine butter, garlic and yolks in a small mixing bowl. Whisk until well combined. Lay potato slices overlapping each other over the base of prepared tin. Brush liberally with butter mixture. Top with a few onion rings and sprinkle with combined breadcrumbs, cheese and pepper.
3 Repeat this layering process until all ingredients are used, finishing with

a breadcrumb and cheese layer. Bake for 40 minutes. Increase oven temperature to moderately hot 210°C, bake a further 10 minutes. Allow to stand 10 minutes in tin before transferring to a board. Carefully remove cake from tin. Cut into wedges and serve.

COOK'S FILE

Storage time: This dish can be eaten hot or cold. Prepare several hours in advance and bake just prior to serving.
Variation: For a different flavour add chopped shallots and a little chopped fresh rosemary to the potato layers before cooking.
Note: Serve with a green salad.

*Salmon Cutlets with Vanilla Glaze
and Onion Potato Cake.*

SALMON CUTLETS WITH VANILLA GLAZE

Preparation time: 40 minutes
Cooking time: 30 minutes
Serves 6

6 (about 200 g) salmon cutlets
1/4 cup lemon juice
2 tablespoons water
50 g butter, chopped
2 tablespoons finely chopped
    fresh chives

Vanilla Glaze
1 cup white wine vinegar

1/4 cup water
1 vanilla bean
1 tablespoon brown sugar
2 tablespoon sugar
1 teaspoon grated lemon rind

➤ PREHEAT OVEN to moderate 180°C. Remove any scales from fish.

1 Place salmon cutlets in one layer in a large baking dish. Pour over combined lemon juice and water; top with chopped butter.

2 Cover with foil; bake 20 minutes or until fish can be easily flaked with a fork. Place on serving plates, sprinkle on chives and spoon on glaze. Serve immediately with Onion Potato Cake.

3 To make Vanilla Glaze: Combine all ingredients in medium heavy-based pan. Stir over low heat without boiling until sugar has dissolved. Bring to boil, reduce heat, simmer for 5 minutes or until glaze has reduced by half. Remove from heat. Discard vanilla bean.

COOK'S FILE

Storage time: Cook this dish just before serving.

Note: Vanilla beans are available from health food shops or delicatessens. If salmon cutlets are unavailable, use rainbow trout fillets or your favourite fish.

ONION POTATO CAKE

Preparation time: 40 minutes
Cooking time: 50 minutes
Makes one 17 cm round cake

4 large potatoes
1 large Spanish onion
100 g butter, melted
2 cloves garlic, crushed
2 egg yolks
1/2 cup fine, dry breadcrumbs
3/4 cup grated parmesan cheese
cracked black pepper
    to taste

➤ PREHEAT OVEN to moderate 180°C. Line a deep, 17 cm round springform tin with melted butter or oil. Line base and sides with paper; grease paper.

1 Using a sharp knife, cut potatoes and onion into very thin slices.

2 Combine butter, garlic and yolks in a small mixing bowl. Whisk until well combined. Lay potato slices overlapping each other over the base of prepared tin. Brush liberally with butter mixture. Top with a few onion rings and sprinkle with combined breadcrumbs, cheese and pepper.

3 Repeat this layering process until all ingredients are used, finishing with

a breadcrumb and cheese layer. Bake for 40 minutes. Increase oven temperature to moderately hot 210°C, bake a further 10 minutes. Allow to stand 10 minutes in tin before transferring to a board. Carefully remove cake from tin. Cut into wedges and serve.

COOK'S FILE

Storage time: This dish can be eaten hot or cold. Prepare several hours in advance and bake just prior to serving.

Variation: For a different flavour add chopped shallots and a little chopped fresh rosemary to the potato layers before cooking.

Note: Serve with a green salad.

*Salmon Cutlets with Vanilla Glaze
and Onion Potato Cake.*

CHOCOLATE AND MASCARPONE TORTE

Preparation time: 1 hour + 30 minutes
Cooking time: 45 minutes
Makes one 20 cm round cake

125 g butter
½ cup caster sugar
½ cup icing sugar, sifted
2 eggs, lightly beaten
1 teaspoon vanilla essence
2 tablespoons instant coffee
  powder
1 teaspoon hot water
1½ cups self-raising flour
½ cup cocoa powder
1 teaspoon bicarbonate of soda
1 cup buttermilk
1 tablespoon vegetable oil

Filling
1½ cups cream, whipped to
  stiff peaks
¼ cup icing sugar, sifted
1 teaspoon vanilla essence
250 g mascarpone

Chocolate Collar
100g dark compound chocolate,
  chopped
2 teaspoons cocoa powder, extra
2 teaspoons drinking chocolate

➤ PREHEAT OVEN to moderate 180°C. Brush a deep, 20 cm round cake tin with melted butter or oil. Line base and sides with paper; grease paper.
1. Using electric beaters, beat butter and sugars in small mixing bowl until light and creamy. Add eggs gradually, beating thoroughly after each addition. Add essence and combined coffee powder and water; beat until well combined. Transfer mixture to a large mixing bowl. Using a metal spoon, fold in dry ingredients alternately with liquids. Stir until just combined and the mixture is smooth.
2 Pour mixture into prepared tin; smooth surface. Bake 45 minutes or until skewer comes out clean when inserted in centre of cake. Leave cake in tin 10 minutes before turning onto wire rack to cool.
3 To make Filling: Combine all ingredients in mixing bowl. Using a metal spoon, fold together until mixture is smooth and free of lumps.
4 To assemble cake: Using a serrated knife, cut cake crossways into three even layers. Place first cake layer on serving plate. Spread evenly with one-third of the filling. Continue layering cake with remaining cake and one-third of filling, with cake layer on top.
5 To make Chocolate Collar: Place dark chocolate in a small heatproof bowl. Stand over pan of simmering water and stir until chocolate has melted and is smooth. Cool slightly. Spread chocolate evenly over a 70 x 7.5 cm strip of baking paper using a flat-bladed knife. Allow to semi-set. Smooth surface.
6 When chocolate is firm enough to stand, but soft enough to bend, wrap the chocolate collar around the cake and seal ends together. Pour remaining filling on top. Smooth surface. Allow to completely set. Peel off paper. Dust the top of cake with combined sifted cocoa and drinking chocolate.

COOK'S FILE

Storage time: Make the cake one day ahead. Assemble on day of serving.
Hint: Mascarpone is similar to soft cream cheese and sour cream. It is available in tubs from delicatessens and selected supermarkets.
Variation: For a marbled collar, melt 60 g white chocolate and spoon it alternately with dark chocolate onto paper strip. Make swirl lines with fork.

BRASSERIE-STYLE

APPETISER: Caraway Pikelets with Smoked Trout

ENTRÉE: Warm Goat Cheese Salad

MAIN: Lamb Cutlets with Tomato-mint Relish

ACCOMPANIMENT: Green Bean Salad

DESSERT: Chestnut Truffle Terrine

CARAWAY PIKELETS WITH SMOKED TROUT

Preparation time: 15 minutes
Cooking time: 20 minutes
Makes 30

½ cup wholemeal self-raising
    flour
½ teaspoon caraway seeds
15 g butter, melted
1 egg, lightly beaten
⅓ cup milk
30 g butter, extra
2 tablespoons soft cream cheese
100 g smoked trout slices
1 lemon, cut in 6, to serve

➤ SIFT FLOUR into a medium mixing bowl; return husks to bowl.
1 Add caraway seeds. Make a well in the centre. Whisk melted butter, egg and milk together and add to dry ingredients. Using a wooden spoon, stir until well combined; do not overbeat.
2 Grease a large heavy-based pan with a little of the extra butter. Allow one teaspoon of mixture for each pikelet, cooking four or five at a time. Cook until bubbles appear on surface, turn to brown other side. Cool on wire rack. Repeat until all mixture is used.
3 To assemble, spread a little cream cheese on each pikelet; top with a piece of smoked trout. Make piles of four or five on each plate. Garnish with a sprig of dill or parsley and a piece of lemon. Serve at room temperature.

COOK'S FILE

Storage time: Pikelet batter can be made one day in advance. Store, covered, in refrigerator. Cook and assemble dish just before serving.
Wine suggestions: A mellow chardonnay, chilled, goes very well with smoked fish, and could be drunk throughout this meal. On a richer note, try a liqueur muscat with dessert.

Lamb Cutlets with Tomato-mint Relish (top), Warm Goat Cheese Salad and Caraway Pikelets with Smoked Trout.

WARM GOAT CHEESE SALAD

Preparation time: 15 minutes
Cooking time: 15 minutes
Serves 6

6 slices wholemeal bread
2 x 100 g rounds goat cheese
100 g mixed salad leaves
1 tablespoon tarragon vinegar
3 tablespoons olive oil
½ teaspoon wholegrain mustard

➤ PREHEAT OVEN to moderate 180°C.

1 Using a biscuit cutter, cut a round out of each slice of bread that will just fit the round of goat cheese. The bread must not extend out from the cheese or it will burn. Place bread onto a baking tray, and cook for 10 minutes.

2 Cut each cheese into three discs. Place a disc of cheese onto each bread round. Arrange a bed of salad leaves on small serving plates.

3 Cook cheese under a hot grill for 5 minutes or until it turns golden and bubbles. Drizzle salad leaves with dressing, place a cheese round on top and serve immediately.

To make dressing: Combine vinegar, oil and mustard in a small jar. Screw lid on tightly; shake vigorously for 1 minute or until well combined.

COOK'S FILE

Storage time: Make this dish just before serving.

Note: Goat cheese is available in large supermarkets and delicatessens. It is usually sold in a round or log shape.

1

2

3

LAMB CUTLETS WITH TOMATO-MINT RELISH

Preparation time: 20 minutes +
   1 hour standing
Cooking time: 15 minutes
Serves 6

12 lamb cutlets, about 70 g each
1 tablespoon olive oil

Tomato-mint Relish
3 medium tomatoes
2 teaspoons brown sugar
1 tablespoon cider vinegar
1 spring onion, finely chopped
2 teaspoons finely chopped
   fresh mint

➤ TRIM EXCESS FAT and sinew from each cutlet.

1 Using a small sharp knife scrape bone until it is clean, and trim meat to a neat disc. Heat oil in pan. Cook cutlets over high heat 2 minutes each side to seal, then a further minute each side. Serve with Tomato-mint Relish.

2 To make Tomato-mint Relish: Mark a small cross on the top of each tomato. Place in boiling water for 1-2 minutes, then plunge immediately into cold water. Remove and peel skin down from the cross. Cut tomatoes in half and gently squeeze seeds out. Remove any remaining seeds with a teaspoon. Chop tomatoes finely.

3 Combine tomatoes, sugar, vinegar and onion in a small pan over medium heat. Bring to boil, reduce heat slightly and simmer 5 minutes. Remove from heat, transfer to a small bowl and leave at room temperature for at least 1 hour. Stir in mint just before serving.

COOK'S FILE

Storage time: Prepare this dish just before serving.

GREEN BEAN SALAD

Preparation time: 20 minutes
Cooking time: 3 minutes
Serves 6

310 g can butter (cannellini)
  beans
2 tablespoons lemon juice
¼ cup olive oil
1 clove garlic, crushed
150 g fresh green beans

➤ DRAIN BUTTER BEANS.

1 Place beans in food processor. Using the pulse action, press button 1 minute or until mixture is smooth.

2 Place juice, oil and garlic in a small jar. Screw top on tightly and shake vigorously for 1 minute or until combined. Add 2 tablespoons of the juice mixture to the butter bean purée and process briefly to combine. Refrigerate, covered, until required.

3 Top and tail green beans. Place in a medium pan; just cover with water.

Bring to boil; cook 3 minutes or until tender. Plunge into cold water, drain. Pat dry with absorbent paper. Place green beans in a medium mixing bowl and toss with remaining dressing.

To serve, pile beans on serving plates and top with two level tablespoons of bean purée. Serve with Lamb Cutlets with Tomato-mint Relish.

COOK'S FILE

Storage time: Make purée one day ahead. Cook beans just before serving.

CHESTNUT TRUFFLE TERRINE

Preparation time: 20 minutes +
   1½ hours refrigeration
Cooking time: 15 minutes
Serves 6

1 cup unsweetened chestnut
   purée
1 tablespoon sugar
20 g butter, softened
200 g dark chocolate, chopped
⅓ cup cream
70 g white chocolate, chopped
1 tablespoon cream, extra

➤ LINE A 15 x 8 cm or 2-cup capacity mini-loaf tin with foil.
1 Place chestnut purée, sugar and butter in medium mixing bowl. Using electric beaters, beat until light and creamy. Cover with plastic wrap; leave at room temperature until required.

2 Place dark chocolate and cream in a small heatproof bowl. Stand over a pan of simmering water, stir until chocolate has melted and mixture is smooth. Remove from heat; cool slightly. Pour half the chocolate mixture into the prepared tin and gently tap tin on benchtop to eliminate air bubbles and level surface. Refrigerate until set. Cover remaining mixture with plastic wrap and leave at room temperature until required.
3 Place white chocolate and extra cream in a small heatproof bowl. Stand over pan of simmering water, stir until chocolate has melted and mixture is smooth. Remove from heat, cool slightly. Spread over dark chocolate layer in tin. Gently tap tin on benchtop to level the surface. Refrigerate until set.
4 Spread chestnut mixture in an even layer on top of white chocolate. Refrigerate. Gently reheat remaining dark chocolate mixture. Spread onto chestnut layer and refrigerate until set.

To serve, cut terrine into 12 thin slices; place two slices on each plate, with fresh seasonal fruit such as mango, kiwifruit or berries.

COOK'S FILE

Storage time: Prepare this dish up to two days ahead. Store in refrigerator.
Hint: To make cutting easier, hold knife under a hot tap, dry thoroughly and slice. Repeat between slices to ensure a clean cut.

TRADITIONAL FAVOURITES

ENTRÉE: Watercress Soup

MAIN: Redcurrant-glazed Roast Turkey

ACCOMPANIMENT: Golden Roast Potatoes

DESSERT: Ice-cream Fruit Bombe

SWEET TREAT: Mini Choc-rum Puddings

WATERCRESS SOUP

Preparation time: 40 minutes
Cooking time: 15 minutes
Serves 8

1 large onion
4 spring onions
450 g watercress
100 g butter
1/3 cup plain flour
2 1/4 cups chicken stock
2 cups water
sour cream, to serve

➤ ROUGHLY CHOP onion, spring onions and watercress.

1 Heat butter in a large heavy-based pan; add onions and watercress. Stir over low heat for 3 minutes or until vegetables have softened. Add flour; stir until well combined.

2 Add combined stock and water gradually to pan, stirring until mixture is smooth. Stir constantly over medium heat for 10 minutes or until mixture boils and thickens; boil 1 minute further; remove from heat. Set aside to cool.

3 Place mixture in small batches in food processor bowl. Using the pulse action, press button for 15 seconds or until mixture is smooth. Return soup to large pan. Gently heat through. Serve warm with a dollop of sour cream on top.

COOK'S FILE

Storage time: This dish can be made up to one week in advance and frozen.
Variation: One small leek can replace spring onions in this recipe.
Hint: Wash watercress well before chopping, as it can harbour tiny snails.
Wine suggestions: This special-occasion menu calls for a wine to partner each course. Before dinner serve a glass of very fine sherry; with the soup, a Rhine riesling or chablis.

Redcurrant-glazed Roast Turkey with Golden Roast Potatoes (top) and Watercress Soup.

REDCURRANT-GLAZED ROAST TURKEY

Preparation time: 1 hour 30 minutes
Cooking time: 2 hours
Serves 8

2.8 kg turkey buffe
¼ cup redcurrant jelly
2 tablespoons golden syrup
¼ cup brown sugar
40 g butter, melted
1 cup water

Gravy
2 tablespoons plain flour
¾ cup chicken stock

Apple Stuffing
20 g butter
1 medium onion, finely chopped
1 large green apple, finely chopped
2 spring onions, finely chopped
4 slices dry bread, grated
1 tablespoon chopped chives
2 teaspoons lemon juice

➤ PREHEAT OVEN to 180°C. Trim turkey of excess fat. Combine jelly, syrup and sugar in small mixing bowl. Stir until smooth.

1 Brush turkey all over with melted butter; place on a roasting rack in a deep baking dish. Pour water into base of dish. Cover with foil and bake 40 minutes. Remove from oven; brush liberally with jelly mixture. Bake uncovered for a further 20 minutes. Repeat process once more. Remove from oven, transfer turkey to a carving board and leave, covered with foil, in a warm place 10 minutes before slicing.

2 To make Gravy: Sprinkle flour evenly over an oven tray. Place under hot grill until flour is golden. Add flour to pan juices, stir over low heat for 2 minutes. Add stock gradually to pan, stirring until mixture is smooth. Stir constantly over medium heat for 5 minutes or until mixture boils and thickens; boil further 1 minute; remove from heat. Serve hot with turkey.

3 To make Apple Stuffing: Heat butter in a medium, heavy-based pan. Add onion and apple, stir over medium heat until golden brown. Add remaining ingredients, stir until well combined. Serve hot with turkey.

COOK'S FILE

Storage time: The stuffing can be made several hours in advance.
Wine suggestions: A soft, full-bodied shiraz complements turkey.

GOLDEN ROAST POTATOES

Preparation time: 20 minutes
Cooking time: 1 hour
Serves 8

8 medium potatoes
50 g butter, melted
¼ cup olive oil
½ teaspoon paprika

➤ PREHEAT OVEN to 200°C. Wash and peel potatoes.

1 Boil potatoes for 5 minutes; drain. Pat dry using absorbent paper.

2 Using the prongs of a fork, scrape the potatoes to form a rough surface. Place potatoes in a shallow baking dish. Brush liberally with combined butter and oil. Sprinkle with paprika. Bake for 20 minutes.

3 Remove from oven; brush with butter mixture. Return to oven for further 20 minutes. Repeat this process again and bake for a further 15 minutes, then serve hot with Redcurrant-glazed Roast Turkey.

COOK'S FILE

Storage time: Make this dish just before serving.
Hint: Use even-sized, old floury potatoes for best results when baking.
Variation: Substitute rosemary for paprika in this recipe if liked.

Redcurrant-glazed Roast Turkey (top) with Golden Roast Potatoes and Apple Stuffing.

ICE-CREAM FRUIT BOMBE

Preparation time: 20 minutes +
  overnight soaking +
  overnight freezing
Cooking time: Nil
Serves 8

310 g jar fruit mince
½ cup dried figs, finely chopped
¼ cup rum
1 cup (80 g) flaked almonds
4 eggs
1 cup caster sugar
1½ cups cream
¾ cup buttermilk

➤ COMBINE FRUIT MINCE, figs and rum in a small mixing bowl. Cover with plastic wrap; allow fruit to soak overnight. Place almonds on oven tray. Toast under hot grill until golden.

1 Using electric beaters, beat eggs in large mixing bowl for 5 minutes or until thick and pale.

2 Add sugar gradually, beating constantly until dissolved and mixture is pale yellow and glossy. Gradually add combined cream and buttermilk; beat for a further 5 minutes.

3 Using a metal spoon, fold in fruit mixture and almonds. Pour mixture into a deep 8-cup capacity pudding bowl and cover with foil. Place in freezer. Allow to freeze overnight.

4 To remove pudding from bowl, push a flat-bladed knife down between bowl and pudding to allow air in.

Gently ease pudding onto serving plate; garnish with extra figs and almonds. Cut into wedges to serve.

COOK'S FILE

Storage time: Prepare one day ahead.
Wine suggestions: Try a sweet dessert wine or sweet champagne.

MINI CHOC-RUM PUDDINGS

Preparation time: 50 minutes +
refrigeration
Cooking time: 5 minutes
Makes about 20

250 g moist chocolate cake,
  crumbled
¼ cup ground nuts
1 tablespoon golden syrup
1 tablespoon overproof rum
50 g butter, melted
½ cup fruit mince
150 g dark chocolate, chopped
15 g white vegetable shortening
60 g white chocolate, chopped
1 tablespoon cream

➤ COMBINE CAKE CRUMBS, nuts, syrup, rum, butter and fruit mince in large mixing bowl.

1 Using a metal spoon, stir until mixture comes together. Roll two heaped teaspoons of mixture into balls. Place on a tray; refrigerate until firm.

2 Place dark chocolate and shortening in medium heatproof bowl. Stand over pan of simmering water; stir until chocolate and shortening have melted and mixture is smooth. Cool slightly.

3 Using two forks, dip balls into melted chocolate; drain excess. Place balls on tray. Refrigerate until firm.

4 Place white chocolate and cream in small heatproof bowl. Stand over pan of simmering water; stir until chocolate has melted and mixture is smooth. Cool slightly. Spoon half a teaspoon of

mixture on top of each ball. Allow mixture to run down the sides. Refrigerate until set. Decorate balls with slivers of green and red glacé cherries if desired. Serve with coffee.

COOK'S FILE

Storage time: This dish can be made seven days ahead. Store, covered, in the refrigerator.

Wine suggestion: To finish the meal, serve an excellent old port.

SOUTHERN SPICE

ENTRÉE:	Cornmeal Chillies
MAIN:	Crab Cakes with Hot Salsa
ACCOMPANIMENT:	Coriander Salad
DESSERT:	Frozen Lemon Tart
SWEET TREAT:	Ginger Chocolates

CORNMEAL CHILLIES

Preparation time: 30 minutes +
    2 hours refrigeration
Cooking time: 2-3 minutes each batch
Serves 6

330 g jar mild whole chillies
½ cup grated cheddar cheese
100 g soft cream cheese
⅓ cup plain flour
2 eggs, lightly beaten
¾ cup cornmeal
¾ cup dry breadcrumbs
oil for deep-frying
sour cream, to serve
1 small fresh red chilli, finely
    sliced, for garnish

➤ SELECT 12 large, uniform chillies from jar. Drain well and dry with absorbent paper.
1 With a sharp knife, cut a slit down the length of one side of each chilli.

Remove all seeds and membrane.
2 Combine grated cheddar and cream cheese. Fill each chilli with cheese mixture. Place flour onto a large plate and beaten egg into a small bowl. Combine cornmeal and breadcrumbs in a small plastic bag. Shake well, then pour onto a large plate. Roll each chilli in flour, shake off excess, dip in egg and roll in crumb mixture to coat thoroughly. Refrigerate for 1 hour. Re-dip in egg and re-roll in breadcrumbs. Return to refrigerator for 1 hour.
3 Heat oil in a medium pan. Test oil by frying a small cube of bread; if it browns in 30 seconds, the oil is ready. Deep-fry chillies in small batches until golden; drain on absorbent paper.
To serve, place two chillies and a spoonful of sour cream on each plate. Garnish with a sliver of chilli.

COOK'S FILE

Storage time: Cornmeal Chillies can be prepared up to three hours ahead.

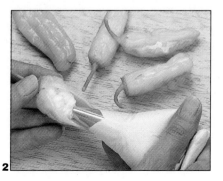

Crab Cakes with Hot Salsa (top), Coriander Salad and Cornmeal Chillies.

1

2

3

4

CRAB CAKES WITH HOT SALSA

Preparation time: 30 minutes +
  30 minutes refrigeration
Cooking time: 5-6 minutes each batch
Serves 6

100 g vermicelli, broken into
  8 cm lengths
600 g crab meat
2 tablespoons finely chopped
  fresh parsley
1 small red capsicum, finely
  chopped
¼ cup finely grated parmesan
  cheese
¼ cup plain flour
2 spring onions, finely chopped
freshly ground black pepper, to
  taste
2 eggs, lightly beaten
2-3 tablespoons oil, for frying

Hot Salsa
2 large ripe tomatoes
1 medium onion, finely chopped
2 cloves garlic, crushed
1 teaspoon dried oregano leaves
2 tablespoons sweet chilli sauce

➤ COOK VERMICELLI in boiling
water until just cooked. Drain well.
1 In a large bowl, combine noodles,
crab meat, parsley, capsicum, parmesan, flour, onions and pepper. Add
beaten egg; mix well.
2 Shape mixture into 12 flat patties;
refrigerate 30 minutes.
3 Heat oil in a large heavy-based pan;
cook crab cakes a few at a time over
medium-high heat until golden brown.
Serve immediately with Hot Salsa.
4 To make Hot Salsa: Combine all
ingredients in a small bowl. Let stand
at room temperature for 1 hour.

COOK'S FILE

Storage time: Crab Cakes and Hot
Salsa may be prepared up to eight
hours in advance and refrigerated until
required. Bring to room temperature
before serving.
Wine suggestions: Spicy food is the
most difficult to partner with wine.
Some people prefer to drink beer or
mineral water with this food. If you
would prefer wine, try a light Rhine or
traminer riesling.

CORIANDER SALAD

Preparation time: 15 minutes +
20 minutes soaking
Cooking time: 1 minute
Serves 6

⅓ cup burghul
½ cup orange juice
1 cup fresh coriander leaves
200 g red cabbage, finely sliced
1 small red onion, finely sliced

½ teaspoon honey
2 tablespoons balsamic vinegar
¼ cup olive oil
1 small clove garlic, crushed
¼ teaspoon Dijon mustard

➤ PLACE BURGHUL in a small mixing bowl.

1 Heat orange juice in small pan until hot; pour over burghul. Stand for 20 minutes or until all juice is absorbed.

2 Place burghul, coriander, cabbage and onion in a large bowl; mix well.

3 Place honey, vinegar, oil, garlic and mustard in a small jar. Screw lid on tightly and shake vigorously until well combined. Pour dressing over salad, and toss to coat. Transfer to serving bowl. Serve with Crab Cakes.

COOK'S FILE

Storage time: Coriander Salad can be made up to one hour ahead.

Note: Burghul (or cracked wheat) is available from delicatessens and some supermarkets.

1

2

3

FROZEN LEMON TART

Preparation time: 40 minutes +
30 minutes refrigeration +
overnight refrigeration
Cooking time: 25 minutes
Serves 6

1 cup plain flour
80 g butter
2 tablespoons ice water
1½ cups sugar
¼ cup cornflour
1¼ cups water
½ cup lemon juice
1 tablespoon finely grated
lemon rind
4 egg yolks, lightly beaten
30 g butter
2 medium lemons
½ cup sugar, extra
½ cup water, extra

➤ SIFT THE FLOUR into a large mixing bowl; add chopped butter.

1 Using fingertips, rub butter into flour for 2 minutes or until mixture is a fine crumbly texture. Add almost all the water and mix to a firm dough, adding more liquid if necessary. Turn onto a lightly floured surface, knead 1 minute or until smooth. Roll pastry until it is large enough to cover base and sides of a 23 cm flan tin. Line tin with pastry, trim edge. Cover with plastic wrap and refrigerate for 30 minutes. Preheat oven to moderate 180°C. Cut a sheet of greaseproof paper large enough to cover pastry-lined tin. Spread a layer of dried beans or rice evenly over paper. Bake 10 minutes, remove from oven. Discard paper and beans. Return pastry to oven for further 5 minutes or until lightly golden. Set aside to cool.

2 Combine sugar, cornflour and water in a medium pan and stir until smooth. Add lemon juice and rind and cook, stirring, over medium heat until mix-ture boils. Reduce heat slightly, add egg yolks, whisking to combine and cook 1 minute. Remove from heat and stir in butter. Set aside to cool.

3 Slice lemons very finely, being care-ful to retain round shape. Combine sugar and water in a small heavy-based pan. Stir over medium heat without boiling until sugar has com-pletely dissolved. Bring to the boil, reduce heat slightly, add lemon slices and boil for 1 minute without stirring. Remove lemon slices from syrup and drain thoroughly. Spread cold lemon mixture into cold pastry shell and cover top with overlapping lemon slices. Freeze overnight. Stand for 5 minutes at room temperature before serving. Serve with whipped cream.

COOK'S FILE

Storage time: Prepare tart one day ahead.
Hint: Use lemon-flavoured syrup as a refreshing drink with mineral water.

GINGER CHOCOLATES

Preparation time: 10 minutes
Cooking time: 5 minutes
Makes about 24

100 g dark compound chocolate
125 g crystallised ginger pieces

➤ LINE A 32 x 28 cm oven tray with aluminium foil.
1 Place chocolate in a medium heat-proof bowl. Stand over a pan of sim-mering water, stir until chocolate has melted and is smooth. Cool slightly.
2 Add ginger to chocolate, stir to combine, making sure ginger pieces are completely coated in chocolate.

3 Place heaped teaspoons of mixture onto prepared tray. Leave to set. Serve with coffee.

COOK'S FILE

Storage time: Ginger Chocolates can be made four weeks ahead. Store in an airtight container in a cool dark place, or refrigerate in hot weather.

Frozen Lemon Tart (top) and
Ginger Chocolates.

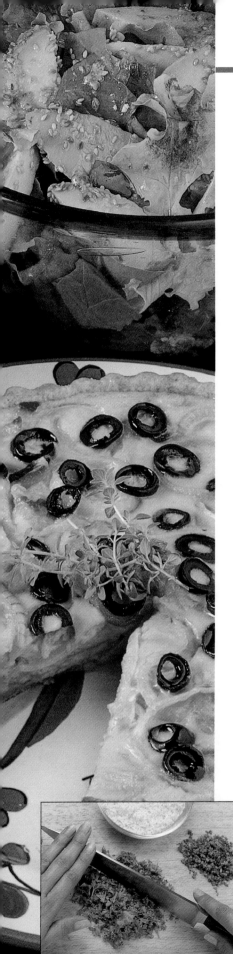

VEGETARIAN DELIGHT

APPETISER: Parmesan-herb Lace Biscuits

ENTRÉE: Mushrooms with Garlic and Red Capsicum Sauces

MAIN: Onion and Olive Tart

ACCOMPANIMENT: Spinach and Avocado Salad with Warm Mustard Dressing

DESSERT: Pecan Blondies with Chocolate Fudge Sauce

PARMESAN-HERB LACE BISCUITS

Preparation time: 10 minutes
Cooking time: 1 minute each batch
Makes 32

75 g parmesan cheese
1 tablespoon finely chopped
fresh parsley
1 tablespoon finely chopped
fresh chives
1/4 teaspoon paprika

➤ FINELY GRATE parmesan.
1 Place parmesan, parsley, chives and paprika in a small bowl and mix to combine. Place level teaspoonful of mixture in flat piles 5 cm apart on a non-stick oven tray. (Cook only a few at a time.)

2 Cook cheese mixture under a hot grill for 1 minute, until golden and bubbling. Watch carefully that cheese does not burn.
3 Let biscuits cool on tray 5 minutes. Lift off carefully with a flat-bladed knife or spatula. Store in an airtight container between sheets of absorbent paper for up to 1 hour.

COOK'S FILE

Storage time: Make these biscuits up to one hour before serving.
Wine suggestions: A rich cabernet sauvignon or a spicy shiraz would go beautifully with this meal. If you prefer white wine, an Australian chardonnay would suit. For a special occasion, you could also serve a sparkling wine or good-quality pink champagne with the appetiser. Finish the dinner with your favourite liqueur.

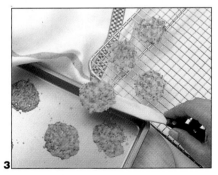

Spinach and Avocado Salad with Warm Mustard Dressing (top),
Onion and Olive Tart and Parmesan-herb Lace Biscuits.

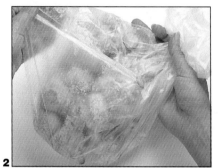

MUSHROOMS WITH GARLIC AND RED CAPSICUM SAUCES

Preparation time: 30 minutes + 1 hour refrigeration
Cooking time: 2 minutes each batch
Serves 8

700 g button mushrooms
1/3 cup plain flour
3 eggs
1 cup dry breadcrumbs
1 small red capsicum
1 cup olive oil
2 egg yolks
1 teaspoon Dijon mustard
1 tablespoon lemon juice
1 small clove garlic, crushed
2 tablespoons plain yoghurt
2 teaspoons finely chopped
    fresh parsley
olive oil for deep-frying, extra

➤ WIPE MUSHROOMS with a paper towel to remove any grit.

1 Place flour in a large plastic bag, add mushrooms and shake until they are evenly coated in flour. Place eggs in a medium bowl and beat lightly. Dust excess flour from mushrooms. Divide mushrooms in half and coat first half well with egg. Repeat with second half.

2 Place breadcrumbs in a large plastic bag. Add half the egg-coated mushrooms; shake to coat in breadcrumbs. Place crumbed mushrooms in a large bowl. Repeat with remaining mushrooms. Refrigerate for 1 hour.

3 Brush red capsicum with a little oil. Grill capsicum until skin is black, then wrap in a damp tea-towel until cool. Rub off skin, and place in food processor or blender. Process to a smooth paste. Place yolks, mustard and half the lemon juice in a medium mixing bowl. Using electric beaters, beat for 1 minute. Add oil, about a teaspoon at a time, beating constantly until mixture is thick and creamy. Increase addition of oil as mayonnaise thickens. Continue beating until all oil is added; add remaining lemon juice. Divide mayonnaise between two bowls. Into one stir garlic, yoghurt and parsley; into the other half stir the capsicum purée.

4 Heat oil in a medium heavy-based pan. Gently lower batches of mushrooms into moderately hot oil. Cook over medium-high heat 1 minute or until golden brown. Remove with a slotted spoon; drain on absorbent paper. To serve, arrange mushrooms on individual serving plates with a dollop of each sauce.

COOK'S FILE

Storage time: Cook mushrooms just before serving; sauces can be made up to one day ahead and refrigerated.

ONION AND OLIVE TART

Preparation time: 1 hour +
30 minutes refrigeration
Cooking time: 1 hour 25 minutes
Serves 8

1 cup wholemeal plain flour
1 cup plain flour
100 g butter, chopped
4-5 tablespoons iced water
1 kg medium white onions
25 g butter, extra
1 tablespoon French mustard
1 cup sour cream
3 eggs, lightly beaten
½ cup thinly sliced black olives

➤ SIFT FLOURS into large mixing bowl; return husks to flour. Add chopped butter.

1 Using fingertips, rub butter into flour for 1 minute or until mixture is a fine, crumbly texture. Add almost all the water, mix to a firm dough, adding more water if necessary. Turn onto a lightly floured surface, knead 1 minute or until smooth. Roll pastry out to fit a 23 cm flan tin. Line tin with pastry, trim edges; refrigerate for 30 minutes.

2 Preheat oven to moderate 180°C. Cut a sheet of greaseproof paper large enough to cover pastry-lined tin. Spread a layer of dried beans or rice evenly over paper. Bake 10 minutes. Remove from oven; discard paper and beans. Return pastry to oven for further 10 minutes or until lightly golden. Set aside to cool.

3 Peel and slice onion into 1 cm rings. Heat extra butter in a large heavy-based pan, and add onions. Cook, stirring occasionally, over medium-low heat 45 minutes. Stir more frequently close to the end of cooking time to prevent burning. Set aside to cool.

4 Spread mustard over pastry base. Combine sour cream and eggs in a medium bowl and whisk together. Spread onions over mustard and pour egg mixture over. Scatter olives on top. Bake for 35 minutes until top is golden and filling has set. Allow to stand for 5 minutes before cutting.

COOK'S FILE

Storage time: This tart can be made up to one day ahead. Store in refrigerator and reheat gently to serve.

1

2

3

4

SPINACH AND AVOCADO SALAD WITH WARM MUSTARD VINAIGRETTE

Preparation time: 15 minutes
Cooking time: 2 minutes
Serves 8

30 (100 g) spinach leaves
1 red curly-leafed lettuce
2 medium avocados

3 tablespoons olive oil
2 teaspoons sesame seeds
1 tablespoon lemon juice
2 teaspoons wholegrain mustard

➤ WASH AND THOROUGHLY dry spinach and lettuce leaves. Tear leaves into bite-size pieces. Place in a large serving bowl.

1 Peel avocados and cut into thin slices. Scatter over leaves.

2 Heat 1 tablespoon of oil in a small pan. Add sesame seeds and cook over low heat until they just start to turn golden. Remove from heat immediately and allow to cool slightly.

3 Add lemon juice and mustard to pan and stir to combine. While still warm, pour over salad and toss gently to coat leaves. Serve immediately.

COOK'S FILE

Storage time: Prepare this dish just before serving.

1

2

3

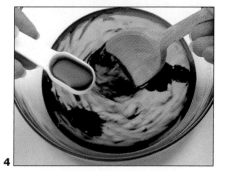

PECAN BLONDIES WITH CHOCOLATE FUDGE SAUCE

Preparation time: 30 minutes
Cooking time: 35 minutes
Serves 8

1 cup self-raising flour
½ cup plain flour
⅔ cup caster sugar
100 g pecans, chopped
125 g butter, chopped
100 g white chocolate, chopped
1 teaspoon vanilla essence
2 eggs, lightly beaten

Chocolate Fudge Sauce:
125 g dark cooking chocolate
⅓ cup cream
1 teaspoon vanilla essence, extra
2 large bananas

➤ PREHEAT OVEN to moderate 180°C. Brush a shallow 27 x 18 cm oblong cake tin with melted butter or oil. Line base and sides with paper, grease paper.

1 Sift flours into large mixing bowl. Add sugar and pecans; make a well in the centre.

2 Combine butter and chocolate in a medium heatproof bowl. Stand over a pan of simmering water, stir until chocolate and butter have melted and mixture is smooth. Cool slightly.

3 Add butter mixture, essence and egg to dry ingredients. Using a wooden spoon, stir until well combined; do not overbeat. Pour mixture into prepared tin; smooth surface. Bake 30 minutes or until skewer comes out clean when inserted in centre of cake. Leave cake in tin 10 minutes; turn out onto a wire rack to cool. To serve, cut crusts from Pecan Blondies. Serve with sliced banana, whipped cream and Chocolate Fudge Sauce.

4 To make Chocolate Fudge Sauce: Place chocolate in a small mixing bowl. Place cream in a small pan and bring to the boil. Pour hot cream over chocolate. Stir until chocolate has melted and mixture is smooth; add essence and combine.

COOK'S FILE

Storage time: Pecan Blondies may be made up to six hours in advance and stored in an airtight container until required. Chocolate Fudge Sauce may be made up to two hours ahead and kept covered at room temperature. Gently reheat over simmering water if sauce becomes too thick to pour.

Variation: You can substitute almonds or walnuts for pecans, if liked.

FEAST ON A SHOESTRING

ENTRÉE:	Red Lentil Dhal with Lebanese Toasts
MAIN:	Spicy Roast Pork
ACCOMPANIMENT:	Stir-fried Noodles with Peanut Sauce
DESSERT:	Apple Galette
SWEET TREAT:	Choc-cherry Squares

RED LENTIL DHAL WITH LEBANESE TOASTS

Preparation time: 20 minutes
Cooking time: 20 minutes
Serves 6

1¼ cups (250 g) red lentils
2 tablespoons oil
1 medium onion, finely chopped
1 clove garlic, crushed
½ teaspoon ground ginger
1 teaspoon ground turmeric
1 teaspoon garam masala
2 cups water

Lebanese Toasts
3 large rounds Lebanese bread
2-3 tablespoons olive oil

➤ PLACE LENTILS in a large bowl and cover with water. Remove any floating particles, drain well.

1 Heat oil in a medium pan. Fry onion and garlic until soft, add spices and stir over a low heat for 1 minute.

2 Add lentils and water, bring to the boil and simmer 15 minutes, stirring occasionally, until all water is absorbed and mixture is thick. Towards the end of cooking time watch carefully that the mixture does not stick and burn. Transfer to a serving bowl and cool to room temperature before serving with Lebanese Toasts for dipping.

3 To make Lebanese Toasts: Preheat oven to moderate 180°C. Cut Lebanese bread rounds into 12 wedges each. Brush with olive oil and bake on oven trays for 5-7 minutes or until light brown and crunchy. Cool on wire racks and store in an airtight container until ready to eat.

COOK'S FILE

Storage time: Make Lebanese Toasts and Red Lentil Dhal up to one day in advance. Store dhal in a covered container in the refrigerator.

Choc-cherry Squares (top right), Spicy Roast Pork, Stir-fried Noodles with Peanut Sauce and Red Lentil Dhal with Lebanese Toasts.

77

SPICY ROAST PORK

Preparation time: 15 minutes
Cooking time: 1 hour 15 minutes
Serves 6

1.2 kg pork neck
2 tablespoons oil
⅓ cup mandarin marmalade
1 tablespoon Chinese five-spice
   powder

➤ PREHEAT OVEN to moderate 180°C.

1 Trim excess fat and sinew from meat. Roll meat and tie up securely at regular intervals to retain its shape.

2 Heat oil in a deep baking dish on top of stove; add meat and brown all over on high heat.

3 Heat marmalade in a small pan over low heat. Add five-spice powder and stir to combine. Brush meat all over with half the marmalade mixture

and bake 30 minutes. Brush with remaining marmalade and cook a further 45 minutes. Leave in warm place 10 minutes, covered with foil, before slicing. To serve, remove string and slice to desired thickness.

COOK'S FILE

Storage time: Cook this dish just before serving.
Hint: Any marmalade, or plum jam, can be used in this recipe.

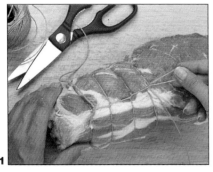

1

2

3

STIR-FRIED NOODLES WITH PEANUT SAUCE

Preparation time: 20 minutes
Cooking time: 15 minutes
Serves 6

200 g broccoli
1 large carrot
3 spring onions
½ cup crunchy peanut butter
¾ cup water
1 tablespoon lemon juice
1 tablespoon Thai sweet chilli
   sauce
250 g fresh thick egg noodles
   (Hokkien noodles)
2 tablespoons oil

➤ DIVIDE BROCCOLI into florets; cut carrot into matchsticks and slice spring onions diagonally.

1 Combine peanut butter, water, lemon juice and chilli sauce in a small pan. Stir over low heat until well combined and mixture thickens slightly.

2 Cook noodles in a large pan of boiling water for 1 minute; drain. Heat oil in a wok or large pan, swirling gently to coat base and sides. Add vegetables and stir-fry over high heat 2 minutes or until just tender. Add noodles and toss to combine.

3 Add peanut sauce. It may have thickened on standing. If so, stir in a little hot water to bring it back to a thick pouring consistency. Toss noodles and vegetables in sauce to coat. Serve immediately.

COOK'S FILE

Storage time: Cook this dish just before serving.
Hint: Thai sweet chilli sauce is available from Asian food stores and some supermarkets. Fresh noodles are also available at Asian food stores.

1

2

3

APPLE GALETTE

Preparation time: 15 minutes
Cooking time: 25 minutes
Serves 6

1 sheet ready-rolled puff pastry
¼ cup bottled apple sauce
3 medium green apples
20 g butter, melted
2 tablespoons soft brown sugar
¼ teaspoon ground cinnamon

➤ PREHEAT OVEN to moderate 180°C. Brush a 32 x 28 cm oven tray with melted butter.
1 Lay out pastry sheet on workbench. Using a plate as a guide, cut a 23 cm circle from pastry. Place on prepared tray. Spread the apple sauce onto the pastry, leaving a 2 cm border around the pastry edge.

2 Peel, core and quarter apples. Slice thinly. Arrange apple slices decoratively over apple sauce, fanning out from the centre of the pastry. Brush melted butter over apple, then sprinkle with sugar and cinnamon.
3 Bake for 25 minutes, or until the edge of the pastry is golden brown. Serve hot, with whipped cream, custard or vanilla ice-cream.

COOK'S FILE

Storage time: Make this dish just before serving.
Hint: Granny Smith apples are excellent for cooking as they soften without losing their shape. Tinned fruit is not suitable for use in this recipe.
Variation: Substitute three large firm pears, or four peaches, for apples in this recipe. If using peaches, dip the whole fruit in boiling water for 10-30 seconds (depending on how big it is).

Lift out and dip into ice water. This process makes the fruit easy to peel.
Note: An economical alternative to a cooked dessert is to offer a platter of fresh fruit with cheese. You needn't offer a huge selection – a piece each of cheddar and blue cheese goes well with nashi pears, grapes or figs. Select the best-looking fruit you can find (take advantage of fruit in season, which will be plentiful and cheap) and arrange attractively on a wooden board or platter. Dried fruit and nuts such as muscatels and almonds also make a good dessert combination.
Wine suggestion: As the idea of this menu is to be delicious yet economical, take advantage of special offers at your liquor suppliers when it comes to choosing wines. A Rhine riesling would suit the slight spiciness of this meal. Red-lovers could try a light red, such as a pinot noir.

CHOC-CHERRY SQUARES

Preparation time: 15 minutes
Cooking time: Nil
Makes 36 squares

250 g dark compound chocolate, chopped
⅓ cup desiccated coconut
100 g red glacé cherries, halved

➤ LINE A DEEP 20 cm square cake tin with aluminium foil.
1 Place chocolate in a medium heatproof bowl. Stand over a pan of simmering water and stir until chocolate has melted and mixture is smooth. Cool slightly.
2 Add coconut to chocolate and stir to combine well. Pour mixture into prepared tin. Tap tin gently on bench to smooth surface.

3 Place cherries, cut-side down, on surface of chocolate. Leave to set, refrigerating if necessary. Using foil, lift out of tin and cut into 36 squares.

COOK'S FILE

Storage time: Choc-cherry Squares can be made up to two days in advance and stored in an airtight container in a cool, dark place or the refrigerator in hot weather.

Apple Galette (top) and Choc-cherry Squares.

QUICK AND EASY

ENTRÉE: Sundried Tomato Dip with Grissini and Crudités

MAIN: Chicken Dijon

ACCOMPANIMENT: Garden Salad

DESSERT: Creamy Mango Grill

SWEET TREAT: Chocolate Glacé Apricots

SUNDRIED TOMATO DIP WITH GRISSINI AND CRUDITÉS

Preparation time: 10 minutes
Cooking time: Nil
Serves 6

150 g sundried tomatoes
2 cloves garlic
1 tablespoon mango chutney
2 spring onions, chopped
6 anchovy fillets
2 tablespoons chopped fresh
    basil leaves
2 tablespoons grated parmesan
    cheese
1 cup sour cream
6 slices prosciutto
12 grissini
vegetables for crudités – e.g.
    baby carrots, celery, broccoli,
    cucumber, red capsicum

➤ DRAIN sundried tomatoes.
1 Combine tomatoes, garlic, chutney, spring onions, anchovies, basil, parmesan and sour cream in food processor bowl. Using the pulse action, press button 40 seconds or until smooth.
2 Cut each slice of prosciutto in half lengthways. Wrap a half-slice of prosciutto around each grissini.
3 Cut selected vegetables into slices; separate broccoli into small florets. Arrange dip and grissini and vegetables attractively on a serving platter.

COOK'S FILE

Storage time: Make Sundried Tomato Dip one day ahead. Store, covered, in the refrigerator. Prepare vegetables and grissini sticks on day of serving.
Hint: Prosciutto, or Parma ham, is Italian air-dried ham. Grissini are crunchy Italian bread-sticks. From delicatessens and some supermarkets.

(Clockwise from top) Chicken Dijon with Garden Salad, Chocolate Glacé Apricots, Creamy Mango Grill and Sundried Tomato Dip with Grissini and Crudités.

CHICKEN DIJON

Preparation time: 10 minutes
Cooking time: 20 minutes
Serves 6

6 single chicken breast fillets
¾ cup whole egg mayonnaise
¼ cup Dijon mustard

➤ PREHEAT OVEN to moderate 180°C. Lay a large piece of aluminium foil over an oven tray. Brush with melted butter or oil.

1 Place chicken breasts side-by-side on prepared tray. Combine mayonnaise and mustard in small mixing bowl; stir until well combined.

2 Spoon the mayonnaise mixture over each chicken fillet.

3 Cover chicken with another large sheet of foil. Fold foil sheets together around edges until well sealed. Bake 20 minutes or until chicken is tender. To serve, spoon juices over chicken. Serve with Garden Salad.

COOK'S FILE

Storage time: Make this dish just before serving.

1

2

3

GARDEN SALAD

Preparation time: 15 minutes
Cooking time: Nil
Serves 6

1 green oak leaf lettuce
1 bunch rocket
1 small radicchio lettuce
1 large green capsicum, cut into
    thin strips
zest of 1 lemon

Dressing
2 tablespoons roughly chopped
    fresh coriander
¼ cup lemon juice
2 teaspoons dark brown sugar
2 tablespoons olive oil
1 clove garlic, crushed, optional

➤ WASH AND DRY salad greens
thoroughly; tear into bite-size pieces.
1 Combine salad greens, capsicum
and zest in a large serving bowl.
2 To make Dressing: Whisk all

ingredients in small mixing bowl
for 2 minutes or until well combined.
3 Pour dressing over salad, stir to
combine. Serve chilled.

COOK'S FILE

Storage time: Make dressing and
salad just before serving.
Variation: Choose a selection of your
favourite salad greens for this recipe.
Wine suggestion: With this light,
summery menu serve a frascati,
chilled, or a slightly chilled light red.

CREAMY MANGO GRILL

Preparation time: 20 minutes
Cooking time: 5 minutes
Serves 6

3 large mangoes
¾ cup cream
2 tablespoons brown sugar
1 tablespoon caster sugar

➤ PEEL MANGOES.
1 Cut mango flesh into thin slices. Arrange slices in six individual ramekin dishes.
2 Pour cream evenly over each dish. Sprinkle with combined sugars.
3 Preheat grill to hot. Place dishes under grill for 5 minutes or until the sugar has caramelised and mango is warm. Serve immediately, with a wafer biscuit or tuille.

COOK'S FILE

Storage time: Make this dish just before serving.
Variation: This recipe can also be made using bananas or peaches. For a richer dessert, add a drop of Grand Marnier to cream.
Wine suggestions: Champagne, either sweet or dry according to your taste, would go well with this dessert.

CHOCOLATE GLACÉ APRICOTS

Preparation time: 45 minutes
Cooking time: 5-10 minutes
Makes about 24

250 g glacé apricots
100 g dark or milk chocolate melts
50 g white chocolate melts

➤ LINE A TRAY with greaseproof paper or foil.
1 Using scissors or a sharp knife, cut each apricot into three.
2 Place dark chocolate melts in a small heatproof bowl. Stand over pan of simmering water and stir until chocolate has melted and is smooth. Cool slightly. Dip apricot pieces one at a time into chocolate to coat only half.

Drain off excess chocolate. Place on prepared tray. Set aside to harden.
3 Place white chocolate melts in a small heatproof bowl. Stand over pan of simmering water, stir until chocolate has melted and is smooth. Cool slightly. Spoon chocolate into small paper icing bag, seal open end. Snip tip off piping bag. Pipe chocolate in squiggles, lines, initials or the design of your choice onto dark chocolate. Allow to set. Serve with coffee and liqueur.

COOK'S FILE

Storage time: Chocolate Glacé Apricots can be made up to three weeks ahead. Store in an airtight container in a cool, dry place.
Variation: Use glacé peaches or pears, or a combination of any of your favourite glacé fruits in this recipe. Fresh dates can also be prepared the same way. Remove the stone first and put a blanched almond or little dried mixed peel into the cavity. Then dip in dark chocolate and decorate with white chocolate as above.
Instead of piping white chocolate as decoration onto dark chocolate, dip the uncoated end of the apricots into the white chocolate. (Increase the amount of white chocolate to 100 g if you want to do this.) Or make a marbled pattern by swirling dark and white melted chocolate together with the handle of a wooden spoon before dipping.
Hint: If apricot pieces are small, use tongs to dip into melted chocolate. These chocolates should set at room temperature. However, if the weather is warm, refrigerate briefly to set.
Wine suggestions: For a grand finale, you could break out the brandy. A sweet fortified wine, such as muscat, tokay or port, also goes well with this after-dinner treat.

Creamy Mango Grill (top) and Chocolate Glacé Apricots.

SEAFOOD BANQUET

APPETISER:	Spicy Almonds
ENTRÉE:	Seafood with Mango Salsa
MAIN:	Tuna Steaks with Olive Paste
ACCOMPANiMENT:	Pasta with Sundried Tomato Pesto
DESSERT:	Raspberry Cheesecake

SPICY ALMONDS

Preparation time: 10 minutes
Cooking time: 17 minutes
Makes 2 cups

2 cups (300 g) whole almonds
2 tablespoons olive oil
½ teaspoon ground cumin
½ teaspoon ground coriander
½ teaspoon garlic powder
¼ teaspoon chilli powder
¼ teaspoon ground ginger
¼ teaspoon ground cinnamon
salt, for sprinkling

➤ PREHEAT OVEN to slow 150°C.
1 Heat oil in a heavy-based frypan. Add cumin, coriander, garlic and chilli powder, ginger and cinnamon. Cook, stirring, over low heat for 2 minutes.
2 Remove from heat, add almonds and stir until almonds are thoroughly coated with the spice mixture.

3 Spread almonds onto a 32 x 28 cm oven tray and cook for 15 minutes. Remove from oven, sprinkle with a little salt to taste and allow to cool.

COOK'S FILE

Storage time: Spicy Almonds may be made up to one day in advance. Store in an airtight container.
Variation: Use cashews, peanuts or any combination of nuts in this recipe.
Wine suggestions: With this very up-to-date seafood meal there is a choice of wines that would suit. Many people favour sauvignon blanc with seafood, and this could be drunk throughout the meal as it would also sit well with dessert, but the strong flavours of olive paste and tuna would also go well with an oaky chardonnay. A lightly chilled pinot noir would also suit. Before the meal offer a glass of champagne or an icy cold beer. Always serve white wine well chilled; an ice bucket is helpful in hot weather.

(Clockwise from top left) Raspberry Cheesecake, Seafood with Mango Salsa, Spicy Almonds, Tuna Steaks with Olive Paste and Pasta with Sundried Tomato Pesto.

SEAFOOD WITH MANGO SALSA

Preparation time: 30 minutes +
   1 hour refrigeration
Cooking time: 3 minutes
Serves 6

1 dozen oysters on the shell
2 medium tubes (about 300 g)
   calamari
10 g butter
1 tablespoon lemon juice
1 tablespoon finely chopped
   fresh parsley
12 medium prawns, cooked,
   left unpeeled

Mango Salsa
1 large ripe mango
1 small fresh red chilli
1 stalk lemongrass
1 teaspoon finely chopped
   coriander
1 teaspoon finely grated fresh
   ginger

Dill Vinaigrette
2 tablespoons white wine
   vinegar

½ cup oil
1 teaspoon Dijon mustard
2 teaspoons finely chopped
   fresh dill
2 teaspoons honey
salt and white pepper to taste

➤ REMOVE ANY GRIT from surface of oyster flesh.

1 Slice calamari tubes into 1 cm rings. Melt butter in a medium frypan, add calamari and lemon juice; stir over medium heat for about 3 minutes or until opaque.

2 Stir in parsley. Remove mixture from pan, set aside to cool. Refrigerate until required.

3 To make Mango Salsa: Peel mango, remove seed and cut flesh into small cubes. Cut chilli in half lengthways, remove seeds and slice finely. Cut a 2 cm piece of the white part of the lemongrass stalk and chop finely. Combine mango, chilli, coriander, ginger and lemongrass in a small bowl and refrigerate 1 hour. Allow to stand at room temperature for 10 minutes before serving.

4 To make Dill Vinaigrette: Place vinegar, oil, mustard, dill and honey in a small jar. Screw lid on tightly and shake vigorously 1 minute or until combined. Add salt and pepper to taste. To serve, divide oysters, prawns and calamari between plates with a heaped tablespoon of Mango Salsa. Put Dill Vinaigrette in a tiny bowl for each plate or pass separately in a small jug.

COOK'S FILE

Storage time: Mango Salsa can be made one day ahead. Cook calamari just before serving.

TUNA STEAKS WITH OLIVE PASTE

Preparation time: 15 minutes +
    1 hour marinating
Cooking time: 4 minutes each steak
Serves 6

⅓ cup olive oil
2 tablespoons dry white wine
2 tablespoons lemon juice
6 tuna steaks (about 200 g each)

Olive Paste
1 cup black pitted olives
2 teaspoons capers
1 clove garlic, crushed
1 tablespoon olive oil, extra

1 tablespoon finely chopped
    parsley
6 teaspoons sour cream

➤ COMBINE OLIVE OIL, white wine and lemon juice in a small jar, screw lid on tightly and shake vigorously for 30 seconds.

1 Place tuna steaks in a single layer in a shallow ceramic or glass dish. Pour marinade over tuna and refrigerate for 1 hour, turning tuna over halfway through marinating time.

2 To make Olive Paste: Combine olives, capers, garlic and oil in food processor and, using the pulse action, process for 30 seconds or until well combined. Refrigerate until required. Allow Olive Paste to stand 10 minutes

at room temperature before serving.

3 Remove tuna steaks from dish, reserve marinade. To barbecue, place tuna on lightly greased chargrill or flat plate. Cook over high heat 2-3 minutes each side, basting occasionally with marinade. Alternatively, cook the steaks on a foil-lined grill under high heat for 2-3 minutes each side, basting occasionally with marinade.

To serve, stir chopped parsley into the olive paste. Place one tuna steak on each plate, top with a level tablespoon of olive paste and a teaspoon of sour cream. Serve immediately.

COOK'S FILE

Storage time: Make this dish just before serving.

1

2

3

1

2

3

4

PASTA WITH SUNDRIED TOMATO PESTO

Preparation time: 15 minutes
Cooking time: 15 minutes
Serves 6

150 g sundried tomatoes in
   olive oil
½ cup finely grated parmesan
   cheese
⅓ cup pine nuts

½ cup fresh basil leaves
⅓ cup olive oil
300 g pasta spirals

➤ DRAIN SUNDRIED tomatoes.
1 Place tomatoes, cheese, pine nuts and basil in food processor. Using pulse action, process for 1 minute or until finely chopped.
2 With motor running, pour in oil in a steady stream.
3 Cook pasta in a large pan of boiling water. Drain well in a colander; place pasta in a large serving bowl.
3 Add sundried tomato mixture to hot pasta and toss to combine well. Serve immediately.

COOK'S FILE

Storage time: This dish can be made one hour ahead and served at room temperature. Sundried tomato pesto can be made up to one day in advance and stored in an airtight container in the refrigerator.

RASPBERRY CHEESECAKE

Preparation time: 25 minutes +
  3 hours refrigeration
Cooking time: Nil
Makes one 20 cm cheesecake

150 g wheatmeal biscuits
2 tablespoons caster sugar
30 g butter, melted
250 g packet cream cheese
1/3 cup caster sugar, extra
1/2 teaspoon vanilla essence
2 teaspoons gelatine
2 tablespoons lemon juice
1/2 cup cream, whipped

2 x 200 g punnets fresh raspberries

➤ BRUSH THE BASE and sides of a 20 cm springform cake tin with melted butter or oil.

1 Place biscuits in food processor and process until finely crushed. Transfer to a medium mixing bowl and add sugar; stir to combine. Pour in melted butter and stir until crumbs are all moistened. Spoon into prepared tin and smooth over base with the back of a spoon. Refrigerate.

2 Using electric beaters, beat cream cheese and extra sugar in a small mixing bowl until light and creamy. Add essence; beat until combined.

3 Combine gelatine with lemon juice in a small bowl. Stand in hot water; stir until dissolved. Add to cream cheese mixture and beat until combined. With a metal spoon, fold in whipped cream, then one punnet of the raspberries until just combined. Pour filling onto prepared base; smooth surface. Arrange remaining raspberries on top; refrigerate for at least 3 hours.

COOK'S FILE

Storage time: This dish can be made up to eight hours in advance. Store, covered, in the refrigerator.
Variation: Replace 1 tablespoon of biscuit crumbs with 1 tablespoon of almond meal.

1

2

3

COUNTRY FARE

ENTRÉE: Stuffed Field Mushrooms

MAIN: Hearty Beef Casserole

ACCOMPANIMENT: Farmhouse Loaf

DESSERT: Apricot Pie

SWEET TREATS: Chocolate Shortbread Fingers

STUFFED FIELD MUSHROOMS

Preparation time: 20 minutes
Cooking time: 10 minutes
Serves 8

8 large field mushrooms
2 medium tomatoes
1 avocado
¼ cup chopped garlic chives
1½ cups cheddar cheese, grated
cracked pepper, to taste
8 slices thick white bread
1 clove garlic, crushed
50 g butter, melted

➤ PREHEAT OVEN to moderate 180°C. Line two 32 x 28 cm oven trays with aluminium foil.

1 Wipe mushrooms with a damp cloth to remove any dirt. Remove stalks. Slice tomatoes and avocado thinly. Turn mushrooms upside down and place a slice of tomato and a slice of avocado on each mushroom.

2 Top with cheese, garlic chives and cracked pepper to taste. Place on one of the prepared trays.

3 Using an 8 cm round cutter, cut out 8 circles of bread. Combine garlic and butter in small bowl. Brush each bread circle with garlic butter; place on other prepared tray. Bake both trays for 10 minutes or until mushrooms are hot and garlic breads are lightly golden. To serve, place each mushroom on top of a garlic bread. Serve hot.

COOK'S FILE

Storage time: Cook this dish just before serving.

Wine suggestions: A robust cabernet sauvignon or claret would be suitable. Decant the wine into a carafe or jug an hour before serving. Because of the simplicity of this country-style meal, it is not necessary to have a different wine for each course.

Hearty Beef Casserole (top) and Stuffed Field Mushrooms.

HEARTY BEEF CASEROLE

Preparation time: 45 minutes
Cooking time: 2 hours
Serves 8

1.2 kg rump steak
4 rashers bacon
½ cup plain flour
1 tablespoon mixed dried herbs
1 tablespoon oil
14 small pickling onions
400 g can tomatoes, roughly
   chopped
1⅔ cups vegetable stock
3 medium carrots, chopped
3 celery sticks, chopped

400 g swede, cubed
½ cup red wine
3 large zucchini, sliced

➤ PREHEAT OVEN to moderate 180°C. Trim meat of any fat and sinew.
1 Cut meat into 2 cm cubes. Cut bacon into 2 cm strips. Combine flour and herbs on a sheet of greaseproof paper. Toss meat lightly in seasoned flour; shake off excess. Reserve remaining flour.
2 Heat oil in large heavy-based pan. Add bacon, cook over medium-high heat until browned; drain on absorbent paper. Add onions, cook over high heat until well browned; drain on absorbent paper. Cook meat quickly, in small batches over medium-high heat

until well browned; lift out and drain on absorbent paper.
3 Transfer meat, bacon and onions to large casserole dish. Add tomatoes and stock. Bake, covered, for 40 minutes. Remove from oven; stir in carrots, celery, swede and combined wine and remaining flour. Cover, return to oven and bake further 40 minutes. Stir in zucchini, bake a further 20 minutes. Serve hot with Farmhouse Loaf.

COOK'S FILE

Storage time: This dish can be prepared up to two days in advance. Store, covered in plastic wrap in the refrigerator. Reheat before serving.
Variation: Add 1 teaspoon of paprika to the seasoned flour.

FARMHOUSE LOAF

Preparation time: 1 hour
Cooking time: 35-40 minutes
Serves 8

7 g sachet dried yeast
2 teaspoons sugar
1 cup warm water
¾ cup warm milk
1½ cups plain wholemeal flour
2 cups self-raising flour
40 g butter, melted
¼ cup plain flour, extra

➤ PREHEAT OVEN to moderately hot 210°C. Brush a 25 x 15 x 5.5 cm loaf tin with melted butter or oil.
1 Combine yeast and sugar in a bowl. Gradually add combined water and milk; blend until smooth. Stand, covered with plastic wrap, in warm place 10-15 minutes or until foamy.
2 Sift flours into large mixing bowl. Make a well in the centre, add butter and yeast mixture. Using a knife, mix to form a soft dough. Turn the dough onto a lightly floured surface, knead for 5 minutes or until smooth. Shape dough into a ball, place in large, lightly

oiled mixing bowl. Cover and leave in a warm place 15 minutes or until well risen. Punch air from dough; knead again for 10 minutes or until smooth.
3 Place dough in prepared tin. Leave, covered with plastic wrap, in warm place for 10 minutes or until well risen. Brush dough with milk. Make four large diagonal cuts (about 1.5 cm deep) across the top of loaf. Sprinkle with extra flour. Bake 35 minutes or until browned and cooked through.
4 Stand 10 minutes in tin before transferring to wire rack to cool. Break into pieces or slice to serve.

Farmhouse Loaf (top) and Hearty Beef Casserole.

APRICOT PIE

Preparation time: 40 minutes
Cooking time: 35 minutes
Makes one 23 cm round pie

2½ cups plain flour
¼ cup self-raising flour
⅔ cup cornflakes
250 g unsalted butter, chopped
2 tablespoons caster sugar
½ cup milk
1 egg, lightly beaten
2 x 425 g cans apricot pie filling
¼ cup brown sugar
1 egg yolk
1 tablespoon water
1-2 tablespoons sugar

➤ PREHEAT OVEN to moderate 180°C. Brush a 23 cm round pie plate with melted butter or oil.

1 Place flours, cornflakes and butter in food processor bowl; add sugar. Using the pulse action, press button for 15 seconds or until mixture is a fine crumbly texture. Add combined milk and egg, process 15-20 seconds or until mixture comes together. Leave, covered with plastic wrap, in the refrigerator 10 minutes. Roll two-thirds of pastry between two sheets of plastic wrap or baking paper, large enough to cover the base and sides of prepared plate.

2 Sprinkle brown sugar over pastry base, top with apricot; smooth surface. Roll remaining pastry to fit over the top of pie. Brush pastry edges with combined yolk and water, gently press together to seal. Trim edges. Brush the surface of the pie with yolk mixture.

3 Roll leftover pastry out to 2.5 mm. Using a 1.5 cm fluted cutter, cut enough rounds to cover the entire rim of the pie.

4 Place rounds overlapping each other around the pie. Sprinkle pie with sugar. Make three steam holes in the top. Bake for 35 minutes or until pastry is golden. Allow to stand 5 minutes before cutting.

Serve with vanilla-flavoured whipped cream or vanilla ice-cream.

COOK'S FILE

Variation: Sprinkle a teaspoon of amaretto (almond-flavoured) liqueur over the pie filling, if liked.

1

2

3

4

CHOCOLATE SHORTBREAD FINGERS

Preparation time: 25 minutes
Cooking time: 35 minutes
Makes 12

100 g butter
¼ cup icing sugar
1 cup plain flour
50 g dark chocolate, chopped

➤ PREHEAT OVEN to slow 150°C. Brush a 26 x 8 x 4.5 cm bar tin with melted butter or oil. Line base with paper; grease paper. Sift icing sugar.

1 Using electric beaters, beat butter and sifted sugar until light and creamy. Using a metal spoon, fold in flour and stir until mixture is smooth.
2 Spread mixture evenly into prepared tin; smooth surface. Using a knife, mark into 12 fingers. Bake for 35 minutes or until pale golden. Leave in tin 10 minutes before turning onto a wire rack to cool. When cool, cut shortbreads into marked fingers.
3 Place chocolate in a small heatproof bowl. Stand over a pan of simmering water; stir until chocolate has melted and is smooth. Cool slightly. Spoon chocolate into a small paper icing bag (see Hint) and seal open end. Use

scissors to snip tip off bag; pipe chocolate decoratively over shortbreads.

COOK'S FILE

Storage time: This recipe can be made up to one week in advance. Store shortbread in an airtight container in a cool, dry place.
Hint: To make a paper icing bag, cut a 25 cm square of greaseproof paper; fold in half to form a triangle. With the long side at the bottom, roll a corner to the centre and tape in place. Wrap the other corner around to the back and tape to secure. Fill with melted chocolate, fold the top over to seal then roll down. Continue recipe as above.

OUTDOOR PLEASURES

APPETISER: Port and Pepper Pâté with Moon Toasts

ENTRÉE: Herbed Scallop Kebabs

MAIN: Steak with Coriander Butter

ACCOMPANIMENT: Fabulous Salad

DESSERT: Lime Pies with Blueberry Marmalade

PORT AND PEPPER PÂTÉ WITH MOON TOASTS

Preparation time: 40 minutes +
   overnight refrigeration
Cooking time: 10 minutes
Serves 8

55 g can green peppercorns
100 g butter
450 g chicken livers, chopped
1 medium onion, chopped
2 cloves garlic, crushed
1/3 cup port
1/3 cup cream
1 tablespoon chopped chives

Moon Toasts
10 slices bread
lemon pepper seasoning

➤ PREHEAT OVEN to moderate 180°C. Line an oven tray with foil. Drain peppercorns.

1 Heat butter in a large, heavy-based pan. Add livers, onion, garlic and port. Stir over medium heat until liver is almost cooked and onion is soft. Bring to boil; simmer 5 minutes. Remove from heat. Cool slightly.

2 Place mixture in food processor bowl. Using the pulse action, press button for 30 seconds or until mixture is smooth. Add cream, process further 15 seconds. Transfer mixture to medium mixing bowl. Stir in chives and peppercorns. Spoon mixture into individual or one large ramekin dish. Refrigerate overnight or until firm.

3 To make Toasts: Using a moon-shaped cutter, cut shapes out of bread. Place on prepared tray. Sprinkle with pepper. Bake 5 minutes or until pale golden and crisp. Cool on wire rack.

COOK'S FILE

Storage time: Make pâté one day ahead. Toasts can be made one week ahead; store in an airtight container.

Steak with Coriander Butter and Fabulous Salad (top), Herbed Scallop Kebabs and Port and Pepper Pâté with Moon Toasts.

HERBED SCALLOP KEBABS

Preparation time: 1 hour
Cooking time: 10 minutes
Serves 8

24 scallops
6 large spring onions, green part only
2 medium zucchini
2 medium carrots
20 g butter, melted
2 teaspoons lemon juice
1 tablespoon white wine
2 teaspoons mixed dried herbs
1/4 teaspoon onion powder

➤ WASH SCALLOPS and remove vein; pat dry with absorbent paper. Cut spring onions in half lengthways, then into 8 cm lengths. Line an oven tray with aluminium foil.

1 Using a vegetable peeler, slice zucchini and carrots lengthways into thin ribbons. Plunge vegetable strips into a bowl of boiling water, leave 1 minute; drain, then plunge into bowl of ice water. Leave until cold; drain. Pat dry with absorbent paper.

2 Roll each scallop in a strip of onion, carrot and zucchini and secure with a small skewer. Repeat this process with remaining scallops and vegetables. Cover exposed skewers with foil to prevent burning.

3 Combine butter, juice and wine in a small mixing bowl. Brush over scallops. Sprinkle with combined herbs and onion powder. Place under hot grill 5-10 minutes or until scallops are tender and cooked through.

COOK'S FILE

Storage time: Scallops can be prepared several hours in advance. Refrigerate, covered, until needed.

Wine suggestions: Serve a cabernet sauvignon or chardonnay with the Port and Pepper Pâté; a crisp young semillon with the Scallop Kebabs and a robust, spicy shiraz with the Rib-eye Steak. A fine Italian spumante would go well with dessert.

STEAK WITH CORIANDER BUTTER

Preparation time: 20 minutes
Cooking time: 5 minutes
Serves 8

8 x 180 g scotch fillet steaks

Coriander Butter
150 g butter, softened
2 tablespoons finely chopped
   fresh coriander
1 tablespoon finely chopped
   mint
1 teaspoon grated orange rind
2 teaspoons finely grated ginger

➤ TRIM MEAT of excess fat and sinew.

1 Secure meat with string or toothpicks to hold its shape. Beat butter in small mixing bowl until light and creamy. Add coriander, mint, rind and ginger. Beat until well combined.

2 Place butter in a log shape on a piece of foil or plastic wrap. Roll up, refrigerate until firm.

3 Place meat on lightly oiled grill or flat plate. Cook over high heat for 2 minutes each side to seal, turning once. For a rare result, cook a further minute each side. For medium and well-done results, move meat to cooler part of the hot plate, cook a further 2-3 minutes each side for medium and 4-6 minutes each side for well done. Slice Coriander Butter into 1 cm-thick rounds. Place on top of hot steaks.

COOK'S FILE

Storage time: Coriander Butter can be made up to one week in advance. Store, covered, in the refrigerator. Cook steaks just before serving.

Variation: Substitute fresh rosemary and garlic chives for coriander, if liked.

1

2

3

FABULOUS SALAD

Preparation time: 20 minutes
Cooking time: Nil
Serves 8

200 g snow peas, sliced
    diagonally
1 large red capsicum, sliced
50 g watercress sprigs
4 leaves oak leaf lettuce
5 leaves white coral lettuce
1 punnet cherry tomatoes

Garlic Croûtons
3 slices white bread
¼ cup olive oil

1 clove garlic, crushed
parmesan cheese, to serve

Dressing
2 tablespoons olive oil
1 tablespoon mayonnaise
1 tablespoon sour cream
2 tablespoons lemon juice
1 teaspoon brown sugar
cracked pepper to taste

➤ SLICE SNOW PEAS and capsicum, wash lettuces and tomatoes.
1 Combine snow peas, capsicum,
watercress, lettuces and tomatoes in
large mixing bowl.
2 To make Garlic Croûtons:
Remove crusts from bread slices. Cut

bread into 1 cm squares. Heat oil in
small, heavy-based pan, add garlic.
Stir in bread. Cook until golden and
crisp. Remove from heat; drain on absorbent paper.
3 To make Dressing: Whisk all ingredients in a small mixing bowl for
2 minutes or until well combined.
Just before serving, pour Dressing over
salad. Stir to combine. Top with garlic
croutons and shavings of parmesan
cheese (made with a vegetable peeler).

COOK'S FILE

Storage time: Make this dish just
before serving.
Variation: Any variety of lettuce can
be used in this salad.

1

2

3

1

2

3

4

LIME PIES WITH BLUEBERRY MARMALADE

Preparation time: 1 hour + 30 minutes
Cooking time: 35-40 minutes
Serves 8

Pastry
¼ cup rice flour
½ cup plain flour
¼ cup ground almonds
2 tablespoons icing sugar
2 teaspoons caster sugar
100 g chilled butter, chopped
1 teaspoon water

Lime Filling
1 tablespoon custard powder
1 tablespoon sugar
¼ cup lime juice
⅓ cup sour cream
¾ cup cream, whipped

Blueberry Marmalade
⅔ cup water
1 cup caster sugar
2 tablespoons lemon juice
1 punnet blueberries
4 cinnamon sticks

➤ PREHEAT OVEN to moderate 180°C. Brush eight ⅓-cup capacity fluted tart tins with melted butter or oil. Coat base and sides with flour; shake off excess.

1 Place flours, almonds, sugars and butter in food processor bowl. Using the pulse action, press button for 20 seconds or until mixture is a fine crumbly texture. Add water, process 10 seconds or until the mixture comes together into a ball.

2 Divide dough into eight. Press evenly into prepared tins. Cut eight small sheets of greaseproof paper to fit pastry-lined tins. Place over pastry; spread a layer of rice evenly over the paper. Bake 15 minutes. Remove from oven; discard paper and rice. Return pastries to oven for further 3 minutes or until lightly golden. Stand pastries in tins 5 minutes before turning onto wire rack to cool.

3 To make Lime Filling: Combine custard powder, sugar, juice, sour cream and cream in medium, heavy-based pan. Stir over low heat, stirring constantly until mixture boils and thickens; remove from heat. Cool slightly. Divide custard evenly between pastry shells. Refrigerate until firm. Serve with Blueberry Marmalade and a dollop of whipped cream.

4 To make Marmalade: Combine water, sugar and juice in medium, heavy-based pan. Stir over low heat without boiling until sugar has completely dissolved. Add blueberries and cinnamon sticks. Bring to boil, reduce heat, simmer 5 minutes, stirring occasionally. Remove from heat; cool.

COOK'S FILE

Storage time: Blueberry Marmalade can be made up to two days in advance. Store in an airtight container in the refrigerator. Make Lime Pies the day of serving.

MOVEABLE FEAST

ENTRÉE: Potted Shrimp

MAIN: Chicken and Ricotta Pie

ACCOMPANIMENT: Summer Salad with Basil Dressing

DESSERT: Golden Glazed Spice Cake

POTTED SHRIMP

Preparation time: 20 minutes
Cooking time: 2 minutes
Serves 8

1 kg cooked small prawns
½ teaspoon finely grated lemon
  rind
¼ teaspoon ground nutmeg
¼ teaspoon cayenne pepper
¼ teaspoon ground allspice
300 g unsalted butter
2 tablespoons finely
  chopped parsley

➤ PEEL PRAWNS and remove veins if necessary.

1 Place prawns, rind and spices in food processor. Using pulse action process 30 seconds or until mixture is coarsely chopped, being careful not to overprocess.

2 Heat butter in a medium pan over low heat until melted. Remove from heat and cool slightly. Skim froth from top of butter with a spoon and discard. Pour clear butter into a small jug, leaving the milky whey at the bottom of the saucepan.

3 Add half the butter and the parsley to the prawn mixture and process briefly to combine. Do not process the prawns too finely. Transfer mixture to a 5-cup capacity ceramic or glass dish, and pour remaining butter over to seal. Refrigerate until required. Serve with melba toasts or crackers.

COOK'S FILE

Storage time: Potted shrimp may be prepared up to two days in advance.

Wine suggestions: Informal summer meals call for a chilled white wine such as a chablis, riesling or a lightly-oaked Australian chardonnay. Alternatively, a wine cooler made from white wine mixed with fruit juice and soda water or sparkling mineral water is also delicious and refreshing. In cooler weather, try a young beaujolais, and in any season champagne goes well with a picnic.

Summer Salad with Basil Dressing (top left), Golden Glazed Spice Cake and Potted Shrimp.

107

CHICKEN AND RICOTTA PIE

Preparation time: 30 minutes
+ 30 minutes refrigeration
+ overnight refrigeration
Cooking time: 45 minutes
Serves 8

1½ cups plain flour
½ cup self-raising flour
100 g butter
4 tablespoons iced water
4-5 (800 g) boneless chicken
    breast fillets
150 g sundried tomatoes in oil
250 g ricotta
⅓ cup cream
1 egg, lightly beaten

➤ SIFT FLOURS into a large mixing bowl.

1 Add chopped butter. Using fingertips, rub butter into flour for 2 minutes or until mixture is a fine, crumbly texture. Add almost all the liquid and mix to a firm dough, adding more liquid if necessary. Turn onto a lightly floured surface, knead for 1 minute or until dough is smooth.

2 Roll out two-thirds of the pastry to fit a 23 cm shallow pie dish. Line dish with pastry, cover with plastic wrap and refrigerate for 30 minutes. Cover remaining pastry with plastic wrap and refrigerate until required.

3 Slice chicken breasts into thin strips. Drain tomatoes and slice into very fine strips. Spread tomatoes over base of pastry; top with chicken. Combine ricotta and cream and spread over the chicken strips.

4 Preheat oven to moderate 180°C. Roll out remaining pastry to fit top of pie. Press edges with a floured fork to seal and trim excess pastry. Brush with beaten egg. Cook for 45 minutes or until top is golden brown. Allow to cool and refrigerate overnight. Serve at room temperature.

COOK'S FILE

Storage time: This pie is best made one day in advance. Refrigerating overnight allows the flavours to develop and blend.

Hint: Sundried tomatoes are available at delicatessens and in some supermarket gourmet departments.

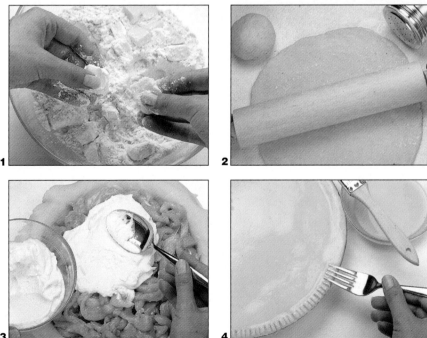

SUMMER SALAD WITH BASIL DRESSING

Preparation time: 15 minutes
Cooking time: Nil
Serves 8

2 medium carrots
6 radishes
150 g snow peas
250 g bunch asparagus
1 cup fresh basil leaves
½ cup olive oil
1 tablespoon white wine
   vinegar
½ teaspoon French mustard
¼ teaspoon sugar

➤ CUT CARROTS and radishes into thin slices.

1 Trim ends from snow peas and cut into 3 cm lengths. Trim woody ends from asparagus and place in a medium pan with a small amount of water.

2 Cook over low heat until just tender. Plunge into cold water, drain. Pat dry with absorbent paper.

3 Place basil leaves in food processor bowl and blend until finely chopped. Add oil, vinegar, mustard and sugar and process until smooth. Store in a jar until required.

Combine vegetables in a large serving bowl. Serve immediately. Pass dressing separately in a small jug.

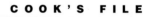

COOK'S FILE

Storage time: The salad is best prepared just before serving. Dressing can be made up to two days ahead.

Variation: Half a cup of coriander could be substituted for half the basil in the dressing, if liked. Cherry tomatoes make a colourful addition to this salad (halve them if they're large). Lettuce, torn into bite-sized pieces, would also be suitable.

1

2

3

GOLDEN GLAZED SPICE CAKE

Preparation time: 20 minutes
Cooking time: 45 minutes
Makes one 20 cm ring cake

1⅓ cups self-raising flour
⅔ cup plain flour
1 teaspoon ground ginger
1 teaspoon ground cinnamon
1 teaspoon ground cardamom
½ teaspoon ground cloves
125 g butter
1 cup soft brown sugar

1 cup buttermilk
2 eggs, lightly beaten
½ cup apricot jam

➤ BRUSH A DEEP 20 cm baba tin with melted butter or oil.

1 Coat base and sides evenly with flour; shake off excess. Preheat oven to moderate 180°C. Sift flours and spices into a large mixing bowl. Make a well in the centre. Combine butter and sugar in a small pan. Stir over a low heat until butter has melted and sugar has dissolved; remove from heat.

2 Add butter mixture, buttermilk and eggs to dry ingredients. Using a wooden spoon, stir until well combined; do not overbeat. Pour mixture into the prepared tin; smooth surface. Bake 40 minutes or until a skewer comes out clean when inserted into centre of cake. Stand the cake in tin for 10 minutes before turning onto a wire rack to cool.

3 Heat apricot jam in a small pan over medium heat. Strain through a small sieve, then brush hot jam onto cake. Serve with thick cream.

COOK'S FILE

Storage time: Golden Glazed Spice Cake is best made on day of serving.

INDEX

Left margin ruler: 1 cm, 2 cm, 3 cm, 4 cm, 5 cm, 6 cm, 7 cm, 8 cm, 9 cm, 10 cm, 11 cm, 12 cm, 13 cm, 14 cm, 15 cm, 16 cm, 17 cm, 18 cm, 19 cm, 20 cm, 21 cm, 22 cm, 23 cm, 24 cm, 25 cm

USEFUL INFORMATION

All our recipes are thoroughly tested in the *Family Circle* Test Kitchen. Standard metric measuring cups and spoons approved by Standards Australia are used in the development of our recipes. All cup and spoon measurements are level. We have used eggs with an average weight of 60 g each in all recipes. Can sizes vary from manufacturer to manufacturer and between countries; use the can size closest to the one suggested in the recipe.

Australian Metric Cup and Spoon Measures

For dry ingredients, the standard set of metric measuring cups consists of 1 cup, ½ cup, ⅓ cup and ¼ cup sizes.

For measuring liquids, a transparent, graduated measuring jug is available in a 250 mL cup or a 1 litre jug.

The basic set of metric spoons, used to measure both dry and liquid ingredients, is made up of 1 tablespoon, 1 teaspoon, ½ teaspoon and ¼ teaspoon.

Note: Australian tablespoon equals 20 mL. British, US and NZ tablespoons equal 15 mL for use in liquid measuring. The teaspoon has a 5 mL capacity and is the same for Australian, British and American markets.

Weights

Metric		Imperial
120 g	=	4 oz
180 g	=	6 oz
240 g	=	8 oz
300 g	=	10 oz
360 g	=	12 oz
420 g	=	14 oz
480 g	=	1 lb
720 g	=	1 lb 8 oz
1 kg	=	2 lb 2 oz
1.4 kg	=	3 lb
1.9 kg	=	4 lb
2.4 kg	=	5 lb

Measures

1 cm	=	½ in
2.5 cm	=	1 in
25 cm	=	10 in
30 cm	=	12 in

Oven Temperatures

Electric	C	F
Very slow	120	250
Slow	150	300
Mod slow	160	325
Moderate	180	350
Mod hot	210	425
Hot	240	475
Very hot	260	525
Gas	**C**	**F**
Very slow	120	250
Slow	150	300
Mod slow	160	325
Moderate	180	350
Mod hot	190	375
Hot	200	400
Very hot	230	450

British and American Cup and Spoon Conversion

Australian	British/American
1 tablespoon	3 teaspoons
2 tablespoons	¼ cup
¼ cup	⅓ cup
⅓ cup	½ cup
½ cup	⅔ cup
⅔ cup	¾ cup
¾ cup	1 cup
1 cup	1¼ cups

Glossary

Australian	British/American	Australian	British/American
Unsalted butter	Unsalted/Sweet butter	Eggplant	Aubergine
125 g butter	125 g butter/1 stick of butter	Plain Flour	Plain flour/All-purpose
Bicarbonate of soda	Bicarbonate of soda/ Baking soda	Self-raising flour	Self-raising/Self-rising flour
Caster sugar	Castor sugar/Superfine sugar	Sultanas	Golden raisins/Seedless white raisins
Cornflour	Cornflour/Cornstarch		
Capsicum	Sweet pepper	Zucchini	Courgettes/Squash

Published by Murdoch Books, a division of Murdoch Magazines Pty Ltd, 213 Miller Street, North Sydney NSW 2060.

Manager Food Publications:
 Jo Anne Calabria
Recipe Origination: Tracy Rutherford,
 Kerrie Ray
Home Economists – Testing and
 Step-by-step Photography:
 Tracy Rutherford, Melanie McDermott,
 Kerrie Ray
Photography: Jon Bader
Step-by-step Photography: Reg Morrison
Editor: Rosalie Higson

Food Stylist: Carolyn Fienberg
Food Stylist's Assistants: Jo Forrest,
 Jodie Vassallo
Publisher: Anne Wilson
Publishing Manager: Mark Newman
Managing Editor: Susan Tomnay
Art Director: Lena Lowe
Project Co-ordinator: Kerrie Ray
Production Manager: Catie Ziller
Marketing Manager: Mark Smith
National Sales Manager: Keith Watson

National Library of Australia
 Cataloguing-in-Publication Data:
 Dinner Parties: step-by-step.
Includes index. ISBN 0 86411 328 5
 1. Dinner and dining 2. Cookery
 3. Menus 641.568
First printed 1993. Reprinted 1994.
Printed by Prestige Litho, Queensland.